TELLI

TELLING IT ALL

A LEGAL GUIDE TO THE EXERCISE OF
FREE SPEECH

Harold W. Fuson Jr.

Andrews and McMeel

A Universal Press Syndicate Company

Kansas City

Library of Congress
Cataloging-in-Publication Data

Fuson, Harold W., Jr.
Telling it all: a legal guide to the
exercise of free speech.
p.   cm.
ISBN 0--8362–7025–8
1. Freedom of the press—United States.
2. Freedom of speech—United States.
3. Journalists—legal status, laws, etc.—United States.
I. Title.
KF4774.Z9F87 1994
342.73'0853—dc20
[344.302853]

94–49146
CIP

Corrections, brickbats, and bouquets can be sent
to the author at PAMSHAL@AOL. COM.

Attention: Schools and Businesses
Andrews and McMeel books are available at quantity
discounts with bulk purchase for educational, business,
or sales promotional use. For information, please write
to Special Sales Department, Andrews and McMeel,
4900 Main Street, Kansas City, Missouri 64112.

CONTENTS

❧ TELLING IT ALL ❧

INTRODUCTION

P RACTITIONERS OF First Amendment freedoms, almost by definition, need not apply for licenses. Americans talk freely, whatever their professional qualifications for the task. Speech professionals, like sex professionals, are more likely than amateurs to meet with legal problems. This book may be skewed toward the problems of the pros, especially journalists, but its goal is to offer practical advice, not only to gallant reporters on prancing chargers, but to the many others, both amateur and professional, whose exercise of their rights to free expression comprises the final bulwark against tyranny and abuse of power. The emphasis is on practice, not theory; on techniques for surviving deadline emergencies, not leisurely lectures laden with legal citations. One legal citation cannot be avoided, however, in any discussion of free speech: Amendment I to the United States Constitution.

A colleague who gives business law advice to media clients once described the task of newsroom lawyers as running into court and shouting "Holy Moly! The First Amendment!" Actually, he didn't say "moly," but you get the picture. Leaving aside obvious sensitivities of some judges for inappropriate crudity, waving the First Amendment flag seldom is the best way to win judicial favor. Most Americans do not know the First Amendment from a fifth of bourbon, and few judges ever grapple with a First Amendment issue of any complexity. Nevertheless, most judges delight in setting aside their calendars of slip-and-fall suits and misdemeanor prostitution cases to indulge in constitutional precedents signed with names like Holmes, Brandeis, and Brennan. In fact, providing relief from judicial humdrum is one aspect of First Amendment law that contributes significantly to the high cost of such cases. ("Take as long as you want, counsel. I've canceled eight drunken driving cases especially to make time for you.")

Not all judges are as accommodating ("Goddamn media think I should drop everything so they can get fifteen seconds on the evening news! Who the hell do they think they are?"). Even those that fancy themselves friends of the First Amendment must be cleared of decades of fuzzy preconceptions ("Didn't Spencer Tracy cite a case for that proposition once?") before good results can be obtained.

Still, the First Amendment remains on the books, and a marvelous presence it is. "Congress shall make no law . . . abridging the freedom of speech, or of the press," it says, after abridging the parts about religion, free assembly, and petitioning the government. Every practitioner of First Amendment–protected activities should copy the full text down on a small card and carry it with the baby pictures in billfold or purse. Here it is:

> Congress shall make no law respecting an establishment of religion, or prohibiting the free exercise thereof; or abridging the freedom of speech, or of the press; or the right of the people peaceably to assemble, and to petition the government for a redress of grievances.

Despite the best efforts of a few Supreme Court justices, the First Amendment doesn't mean quite what it appears to say; either that or journalists aren't as careful in their reading as most justices. Freedom is not "abridged" when a governor denies journalists access to her calendar, though she may have violated a state "open records" law. Shouting "Fire!" in a crowded theater is not "speech." "Freedom of the press" does not include the absolute right to refuse to testify about sources or unpublished information.

For writers and speakers, the First Amendment introduces hurdles and ladders—hurdles that government must get over to punish or limit journalism or speech, and ladders that writers and speakers sometimes can use to achieve goals denied to those engaged in other activities.

Simple reference to the First Amendment cannot determine all the legal rights and duties of writers and speakers. By its terms, the First Amendment is a negative proscription intended by its authors to apply only to the national government and, even there, only to the legislative branch: "*Congress* shall make no law. . . ." Yet, today, all but the strictest constructionists acknowledge that the First Amendment limits all government action, not just the federal legislature. Most also would agree that the First Amendment is not just a negative statement but implies a degree of affirmative constitutional protection for news gathering and speech-related activities.

"The law is a seamless web," law professors pronounce to their bewildered first-year students, and, unlike most first-year lessons, this is a worthy idea. The United States is a federal system with overlapping layers of state and federal jurisdiction. While the First Amendment must be a part of every analysis of the legal rights of writers and speakers, most issues ultimately turn on more mundane matters of *statutory* law (legal principles enacted by legislatures) or *common* law (legal principles set forth by judges in their written opinions—sometimes referred to as "decisional law"), or, occasionally, on other provisions of the federal or state constitutions. Clear thinking about legal rights and duties requires some familiarity with the outlines of the law's web. Appendix A is an attempt at a basic road map. Experienced readers may find it unnecessary; others may want to refer to it before wading into the swamp of libel law.

I

BASIC LIBEL PRINCIPLES

THIS CHAPTER sets forth an analytical framework for solving libel problems. Like a daily dose of roughage, the framework is good for you, but if you start to nod off part way through, skip on to the more scintillating chapters that follow. You can come back to the grander scheme when your mind clears.

DEFINING LIBEL

Those who work under the constant time pressures of a newsroom or hold forth under the gaze of partisan opponents cannot carry around all the nuances of a law school course rattling loosely in their heads. The more they know about the law, the more dangerous they are acting as their own lawyers on deadline. Bringing in a real lawyer often makes the problem worse. Some material—complex investigative news, for example—is difficult to "lawyer" under deadline conditions with little time for calm reflection on legal ramifications. Most news and other information, however, can be handled safely on deadline, if writers and speakers can keep the basic principles clear in their heads. Any number of formulations of these principles will work; what matters is that the deadline gatekeepers have one embedded clearly somewhere in their cerebrums.

Libel may be displayed on the silver screen of the brain in two steps:

- Are the *elements* of libel present?
- If the elements are present, is there a *defense* or *privilege* available?

This approach mirrors what happens in a civil lawsuit. The plaintiff alleges in the complaint that the defendant has done acts that meet the legal definition of a tort. Statutes and court decisions frame this definition as a series of elements. Once a complaint alleging all the elements is on file, the defendant must answer, typically by disputing one or more of the elements and setting forth "defenses"—legal reasons that provide a privilege for the defendant to commit the acts alleged.

First, a closer examination of the elements of libel. Under the definitions followed in most states, the elements fall into four, or even five, groups. However, for nonlawyers working under deadline, it helps to focus on just three:

- Publication
- Identification
- Defamation

A fourth element is *falsity,* a very important element, because it is unprovable by many libel plaintiffs, but also the element most difficult for a journalist or speaker to spot in the heat of debate or under the pressure of deadline. Some lawyers would include a fifth element: a showing of the necessary level of *fault.* For those whose goal is to avoid litigation, falsity and fault are addressed more usefully in the discussion of defenses.

Publication

Publication is the easiest element for the plaintiff to prove in a libel suit against an established publisher. A tear sheet or tape recording is all that's needed. Other issues may arise, however.

Time and Place of Publication

Libel, just like other torts and some crimes, is subject to statutes of limitation that bar bringing a lawsuit after a certain time has elapsed. If the "statute has run" on the first publication, a clever plaintiff may attempt to provoke a second publication, by, for example, having a friend buy a back issue from the publisher. Publishers should make sure that reuse of old material—including redistribution via an electronic database—is as carefully scrutinized for legal problems as was the original publication.

While the statute of limitations may have elapsed in one state, a neighboring state may have a longer statute, inspiring a dilatory plaintiff to hike across the border to file his lawsuit. To do so, however, he must prove that publication occurred in the neighboring state. Many publishers—for example, national distributors of magazines and books or broadcast networks—must assume that their products are published in all states, and be prepared to deal with whatever differing legal principles may be applied in New Hampshire, Louisiana, or California. Even local publications are mailed to libraries and other subscribers in faraway jurisdictions and could be subject to suit in remote locales where plaintiffs may claim that their reputations suffered harm. The differences in law from one state to another usually have little impact on the factors that publishers can control before publication, but these differences can have dramatic impact on the rules that apply in litigation.

Americans also can be sued in foreign jurisdictions where the assumptions embodied in the First Amendment are absent altogether. Traditionally, only a few publishers had to worry about the risks of international distribution, but as trade and language barriers fall, and computer networks reach into every corner of the globe, more and more speakers and writers face these risks.

Form of Publication; Slander

Oral and written statements made to obtain information also can generate legal claims or complicate the defense of suits against published material. The infamous case of the *Alton Telegraph* concerned statements that were *published* only to the United States government in a purportedly confidential memo to investigators, which the reporters wrote to get confirmation of allegations they had heard against a local developer. The memo provoked no response but found its way into government files where later, or so the plaintiff alleged, it played a role in his failure to obtain the credit necessary to keep his business afloat. Even though the newspaper never published an article in its pages, it suffered a multimillion-dollar judgment that helped force the local owners to sell the small Illinois daily to a national chain.

Publication as an element of libel can take any written form, even a scribbled note from a reporter to a news source. While oral communications are not subject to libel suits, they may lead to a slander claim. In most states, the tort of slander differs from libel in only two key respects:

- First, the communication need not be written or recorded, though it must be communicated to a third party. Privately shouting falsehoods to the subject's face is not slander, nor is writing the subject a defamatory letter a libel. So long as no communication is made to a third party, the victim's feelings may be hurt, but his reputation has not been damaged.

- Second, the rules that determine the amount of damages to be paid are much more restrictive in slander than in libel, reducing the incentive to pursue such claims.

As a practical matter, slander claims are more difficult to prove because, by definition, no written evidence of the defamatory statements exists. In some states, claims based on broadcast defamation still are treated as slander, though the more logical course, since most broadcast material is recorded, is to treat such claims by the rules of libel.

Besides the risk that a reporter's "Has your neighbor stopped beating her husband?" questions could provoke a slander claim, speakers and writers must be wary that rashly framed oral statements will be used to paint them as careless scandal mongers. The easiest libel suits to defend are those in which it is possible to portray the writer or speaker as a great servant of the republic who has been consistently careful and unerringly polite. This can be difficult when the plaintiff plays tape-recorded tantrums of the defendant or presents testimony about the unseemly and unsubstantiated gossip the defendant offered to others as bait to attract juicy quotes.

Identification

In most states, the element of identification is phrased as a requirement that the publication be "of and concerning" the plaintiff.

There are many ways to identify a potential plaintiff besides the most direct: "George Washington cheated on Martha." For example, "The first president cheated on his wife."

Members of Groups

Courts are inclined to hold that a general statement about members of a small group ("Supreme Court justices watch smutty movies") identifies every individual in the group. If the group is very large, however, even a very specific statement ("Every lawyer watches smutty movies") will not be held to have identified any one member of the group. Basketball teams, consisting usually of twelve members, are so small that a general statement about "a Bull" or "a Laker" may identify all of them. Football teams, on the other hand, with forty or more members, provide immunity, because of their size, to a journalist who mutters about what "a Ram" or "a Bear" may have done with a bookie on the golf course or an underage person in the backseat of a large vehicle. Woe to the baseball journalist, however, who may not be able to ascertain on which side of the line a group with twenty-five members sits without going through the expensive process of asking a judge.

Capacity to Incur Reputational Harm

To have an action for libel, an identified potential plaintiff must have a nature that is susceptible of reputational damage. Dead persons, for example, are deemed by the law to be beyond reputational damage, though lawmakers and judges in a few jurisdictions have tried from time to time to change this rule. Ethnic groups generally cannot sue for libel, though an incorporated association of persons of a particular ethnicity may be able to sue for damage done to the reputation of the association. The Anti-Defamation League, for example, cannot recoup damages for ethnic jokes or slurs that target Jews, but it could pursue a claim if falsely accused of pursuing a corporate policy of defrauding its contributors.

The immunity of racial or sexual slurs forms the focus for controversies over hate-crime laws and campus speech codes. Such controversies have been stoked by the considerable rhetorical skills of Catharine A. MacKinnon and others who argue that constitutional guarantees of equality ought to override the First Amendment and allow punishment of racially or sexually injurious speech. Whatever the merits of these arguments, which differ hardly at all from those advanced by true believers throughout history, they have to do with what the law ought to be, not with what it is.

Defamation

A *defamation* is a statement of fact so harmful to another's reputation that it will support a libel action. A false and malicious report of the color of a person's hair is not defamatory, because there is nothing about having hair of one color or another that should diminish one's standing with his fair-minded neighbors. Unfortunately, the legal definition of defamation isn't crystal clear, even to judges and lawyers, let alone to writers and speakers.

Defamatory meaning often is muddied up with the concept of "opinion," or, as some courts would have it, the absence of a false statement of fact. This problem is discussed in more detail in connection with the constitutional defense. In short, to be defamatory, a statement must purport to be factual, and a factual statement must be capable of objective proof. "Opinion," as the term is used in its narrow sense to describe a subjective judgment (for example, "mean-spirited"), lacks a statement of fact. An "opinion article" or an "editorial" may contain many factual statements, as well as "opinions," and the factual statements are not immune from a libel action, if the other elements are present and no defense can be established.

A relatively systematic test of whether a statement of fact conveys a defamatory meaning is the statutory categorization of libel "per se" still contained in some state codes, which can be freely translated to cover allegations of any of the following:

- Crime
- Professional misfeasance
- Infection by "loathsome" diseases
- Moral transgressions of a serious order

The dictionary, preferably the one regarded as the office standard, also is a useful reference in testing for defamation. Being able to testify that when you used the word "blackmail" you had in mind *Webster's Ninth New Collegiate Dictionary*'s definition 1, having to do with ancient tributes collected by Scottish chiefs, may help defeat the claim that you were alleging the crime of extortion.

News-writing textbooks sometimes contain lists of "red flag" words that have been held to be defamatory. Such lists can be useful, but only if writers and speakers understand their limitations. Words that some courts have held defamatory, others have held innocent. Words that may be defamatory of a lawyer—"shyster," for example—may be mere hyperbole when applied to a minister. Words that may be defamatory in one era or one context ("Communist" of a 1950s movie actor) may be merely descriptive in another ("Marxist" of a 1980s economics professor). Fine distinctions are never clear until a court rules on them in the context of a specific case, and by then it is too late to rewrite a newspaper article published two years before.

The following examples, taken from recent cases, are intended to provide a feel for how courts have viewed defamatory meaning, not to predict the outcome of future cases:

Alleged Defamation	Court's Ruling
• "[R]acial and religious bigotry."	"[A] subjective judgment incapable of being proved true or false," thus not defamatory.
• "[O]utspoken proponent of political Marxism."	"[L]oosely definable, variously interpretable statement [which is] obviously unverifiable," thus not defamatory.
• "[He] is not married, has chosen an alternative lifestyle that suits him better."	Should be interpreted only as a choice not to marry, not as a defamatory charge of homosexuality.

Alleged Defamation	Court's Ruling
• "We share the concern . . . about possible unnecessary or inappropriate eye surgery."	Not defamatory becaue it lacks "the hidden factual premise that plaintiff was actually performing unnecessary or innappropriate eye surgery."
• Of the producer of cartoon festivals, that he was "not for real," "scamming," and that "there was no such show as [his]."	Defamatory because the statements "implied that [he] lacked integrity in performing his professional duties and also prejudiced him in his business."
• "[Mayor made] repeated and not too subtle attempts to manipulate the press."	After reviewing the dictionary definition of *manipulate*, held that the jury should decide whether the statement was defamatory. A dissenting judge vigorously contended that the statement was not defamatory as a matter of law.
• "A difficult person."	"[D]oes not rise to the level of defamation and would not 'blacken a person's reputation or expose him to public hatred, contempt or ridicule, or injure him in his business or profession.'"
• "[Airline employees' lawyer] compounded the threats of strike, warning that being sold into bondage to [new owner of airline] would provoke night time trashing of airplanes and other sabotage."	"[I]n context is not susceptible to the defamatory meaning that plaintiff supported illegal acts of sabotage. . . ."
• "[A] federal prosecutor says charges are expected to be filed next week against a public works department official."	Accepting argument that "charges" implies criminal and not administrative sanctions, held capable of defamatory meaning.

If the courts' analyses in these examples seem obscure and inconsistent, that is because courts' notions of defamatory meaning often are obscure and inconsistent. In several of the examples, the courts are confused about the difference between defamatory meaning and "opinion." In others, the judgments are at best arbitrary. Defamatory meaning can be divined and avoided, but never with total certainty.

Once it is clear that one or more of the elements of a tort is absent, a lawsuit dies. A writer or speaker worried about the prospect of a libel suit may relax once she ascertains that her desired message is free from identification of a potential plaintiff, or that the facts or criticism she wishes to deliver do not rise, or stoop, to the level of defamatory import.

Nonlawyers working under deadline conditions can test material for identification or defamation. Many lawsuits can be averted, with no loss to the message, by carefully trimming unnecessary or ambiguous identifying details or phraseology that needlessly implies wrongdoing. The problem is that most good journalism and public debate ultimately fails those tests. "Somebody did something wrong at city hall today" is not a prize-winning lead, nor does "I know something smarmy about Mayor Kimble, but I'm not going to tell you what it is" make for a vote-getting stump speech.

Bluntly identifying the wrongdoer and the crime are the keys to advancing truth, democracy, and clear thinking . Such statements lay out the elements of the tort so clearly that the plaintiff need only quote them to state his claim. Stating the elements of a claim, however, is only the beginning. It is then the defendant's turn to give reasons why the law permits her to publish defamatory statements about the good-for-nothing plaintiff.

LIBEL DEFENSES

If all three elements appear to be present, and a statement is about to be conveyed to a third party ("publication") in a manner calculated to tie a specific individual ("identification") to purported facts about his conduct or qualities that would damage him ("defamation") in the eyes of others, then it is time to search for a defense.

The defenses to a claim for libel are numerous and lawyers may state a dozen or more of them in writing an answer to a complaint. All can be loosely grouped into three categories: truth, common law defenses, and constitutional defenses.

Truth

In the deeper recesses of the English common law, truth was not a defense at all. Libel law was a device for protecting the public order and truthful allegations of wrongdoing were more disruptive of public order than false ones; thus, the saying, "The greater the truth, the greater the libel." Fortunately, that notion got lost in the hold of the *Mayflower* and has had little currency in American law, at least since the adoption of the Constitution. The British, in one of their rare gestures toward free speech, have abandoned it as well.

As a matter of legal pleading, truth is no longer a defense but an answer in the form of a denial of the plaintiff's claim of falsity. This is a significant twist; now the burden is on the plaintiff to prove that the statement is false. The problem for the practitioner of free speech is that "burdens of proof" often do not become relevant until a jury is listening. A writer or speaker who is paying the cost of defending himself in a jury trial is already on the edge of pauperdom, no matter what the jury decides. Perhaps, when a well-heeled major publishing company, especially one backed by an insurance company with deep pockets, wins a libel suit by proving truth, it can revel in a glorious victory. The cataclysmic cost of a charge into the valley of litigation death will leave less affluent writers and speakers wrapped in tattered shrouds.

Truth as a weapon in a libel suit is a nuclear deterrent. If you have it on your side, you are less likely to be sued, but if a maniac or a person with nothing to lose decides to push the red button first, Armageddon is upon you. Any trial is likely to cost the salary of one good reporter for at least a year, probably closer to two, and, if a retired general or an oil company chairman is the plaintiff, more like thirty.

Truth has one other shortcoming: hardly anyone knows what it is, and anyone who says he does cannot be trusted. Pete Seeger quotes his father's view: "The truth is a rabbit in a bramble patch. All you can do is circle around and say it's somewhere in there." Even if you disagree with this as a general proposition, imagine yourself trying to guarantee the truth of every word published in the next day's edition of your favorite newspaper, even omitting the classified ads. To avoid wasting their lives in lawsuits, most who wish to bluntly accuse their fellow citizens of felonious relations with barnyard animals need a surer talisman of victory than the hope of convincing a jury that their sheep have been defiled.

The most useful of these predictors of success, those that offer the surest way of knowing that a libel suit, if brought, may be ended merely by asking the court to dismiss it, are found in the next category of defenses.

Common Law Defenses

Every jurisdiction recognizes a group of libel defenses descended from the common law. Most are defined in court decisions, though they may be embodied partially in statutes.

Public Report

One of these defenses towers over the others in its importance to writers and speakers trying to make decisions in the heat of debate or against deadlines. It goes by several names, including the "bread and butter" defense, but it is best described as the privilege of fairly and accurately reporting public proceedings and official acts; call it the *public report privilege.*

First, note the difference between accuracy and truth:

> A lie may be accurately reported, though it is, by defini-
> tion, untrue. An accurate report of an untruth is not privi-
> leged—that is, protected from a libel suit—simply because
> it is accurate.

Tape recorders or Xerox machines, effective as they are in insuring accuracy, are helpful in defense only when used to accurately cap-ture information that already is privileged. The magic quality of the public report privilege is that truth is irrelevant; one who in-vokes it need only establish that the defamatory statement is a fair and accurate report of what was said.

Public proceedings include a wide spectrum of events and doc-uments, but the precise boundaries are hard to identify. You may know that the speed limit is 55 miles per hour, but you aren't sure until you see the flashing red lights whether the speed that pro-vokes a pinch is 67 or 71. Court proceedings, including both hear-ings and the files of court records, generally qualify for protection (though it is always a good idea to see or hear the proceedings yourself, not just rely on a lawyer's secondhand account). Some states exempt the initial complaint from such protection until the other side's response is filed.

Privileged, also, are the proceedings of legislative bodies, rang-ing from Congress to the local water district board. In some juris-dictions, "public" appears to mean just that: any event open to the public, regardless of sponsorship, including an address by a street corner orator or a politician on a stump. The same statements by a politician in a rally open only to party members or at a $1,000-a-plate fund-raiser might not qualify, however, and, if made in a pri-vate interview with a reporter, clearly would not, leaving the re-porter who wants to publish them to find a defense other than public report.

Official acts certainly include announcements by police spokespersons about arrests or other investigative developments and official proclamations by mayors. Muttered speculations by a cop on a beat, or spontaneous curses by an agriculture secretary inadvertently caught by an open mike, are less certain of protection.

"Fair and accurate reports" must accurately capture the substance of the charge and provide the context necessary for the reader to appreciate its limitations. "John Wayne Gacy murdered thirty-three children" may be an accurate statement of a moral truth, but standing alone it lacks the necessary context to qualify for the defense that would be available to: "Gacy was convicted by a Chicago jury of the murders of thirty-three youths." The former purports to be a truthful statement of Gacy's guilt; the latter purports only to be an accurate report of a jury's official act, Gacy's conviction. If Gacy were to sue (not likely, even before his execution, though he did die professing his innocence), the latter statement is much easier to defend.

The news that General Motors knowingly permitted trucks to be built with gas tanks prone to inconveniently timed explosions, especially when that news is illustrated by amateurishly contrived illustrative fireworks, may prompt an expensive libel suit. The same news, without the fireworks, containing clear statements that the charges were from lawsuits on file in numerous courts and that General Motors denied liability, would prompt no libel suit; if it did, the suit could be inexpensively dismissed as a fair and accurate report of a court proceeding.

Neither of the previous examples is intended to discourage calling a shovel by its true name. Gacy could not sue successfully no matter what you called him, and General Motors did sue only because it guessed, rightly, that NBC would be so embarrassed by its own amateur pyrotechnics that it would settle rather than defend the gist of its attack. Precisely tying allegations of wrongdoing to privileged sources makes them easier to defend, and, quite often, elevates public discourse at the expense of pyrotechnics, verbal or otherwise.

The presence of gray areas on the edges takes little away from the huge value of the public report privilege, since so much of the discourse of public affairs rests comfortably inside its 55-mile-per-hour zone. The journalist or citizen who wants to rely on it merely must be certain that the defamatory charges occurred in a privileged setting and that they are reported accurately and in context.

Fair Comment

The defense of *fair comment* is found in some form in all American jurisdictions. Conceptually, fair comment is difficult to distinguish from its constitutional counterpart the "opinion defense" or from an attack on the element of defamation. All three hinge on the absence of an assertion of fact. Unfortunately, the interest in judicial economy always yields to creative litigants who exploit complexity to achieve victory. These three different routes to the same result may seem largely redundant, but so long as some courts are unwilling to accept all three, free speech is served by keeping them all alive.

The crown prince of fair comment is Billy Hamilton of the *Odebolt Chronicle*. Odebolt is in Iowa, as were the Cherry Sisters, a vaudeville ensemble of considerable national reputation. By the time they did their act in Odebolt, however, Effie was spavined and Addie was stringhalt, and they all capered monstrously, or so it appeared to Mr. Hamilton, who said as much about them in the *Chronicle*. When Hamilton's review was reprinted in the *Des Moines Leader,* the Cherry Sisters felt compelled to respond at law. At the trial of their libel suit, they went so far as to perform for the judge to demonstrate the aridity of Billy's appreciation of their art. The judge held with Billy, though it shouldn't have taken a trial to resolve the case. Hamilton's review was a classic case of fair comment: an accurate statement of the facts—to wit, that the sisters had sung in Odebolt—coupled with the reviewer's comment derived from those facts—to wit, that the ladies were not in good form.

The key to the fair comment defense is to get the facts right. Be damn sure it was the Cherry Sisters, not the Indigo Girls, and that what you said was their rendition of "My Gal, Sal" was not an early version of "American Pie."

Fair comment shares a weakness with its descendant, the constitutional defense: It rewards far-fetched obloquy, "spavined" and "stringhalt," at the expense of precision. You can say the pizza tasted like cardboard, but, unless you have witnesses, do not say it arrived twenty minutes later than promised. The time of delivery presumably is capable of factual verification, while the cardboard texture is in the palate of the consumer. Careful, analytical criticism may be more likely to be held to be not comment, but fact, and the critic required to resort to a more expensive defense, like truth, if his statements are so severe as to diminish the performer's professional stature. When fair comment is given a scope consistent with its philosophical basis—that is, that people who offer themselves or their products to the public, must take the heat or leave the kitchen—criticism and consumer journalism are given a wide measure of protection.

Public report and fair comment, unlike truth, are defenses that can be established with confidence before publication under the heat of deadline or debate. Few of the other common law defenses are as useful, because their presence is difficult to establish until after the drink is in you, or, like the defense of consent, are simply not present in most cases. Helpful lawyers may be able to identify such defenses and assist speakers and writers to structure their work to take advantage of them.

Constitutional Protection

"An occasion for dancing in the streets" is how one eminent constitutional scholar greeted the Supreme Court's decision in *New York Times* v. *Sullivan,* the only court decision so awesome in portent that its name must appear in the text of this book and be tucked away in the brains of all serious practitioners of First Amendment freedoms. In *Sullivan,* the Supreme Court announced for the first time that the common law of libel, which predated the enactment of the Constitution by several centuries and had continued to evolve unmolested by federal courts well into the 1960s, could be trumped by the First Amendment.

The Court was unwilling to hold, as two justices thought it should, that "no law" meant "no law" and that the Constitution mandated the abolition of libel. Instead, *Sullivan* raised a constitutional barrier that some libel plaintiffs must clear. This barrier is known by several names, the most common and least enlightening of which is "actual malice." The barrier as announced in *Sullivan* applied only to plaintiffs who could be classified as "public officials." Subsequent court decisions have expanded, polished, and twisted the First Amendment's restraint on libel. These are the present parameters of the constitutional defense:

- To recover damages for libel from a media defendant, any plaintiff must establish that a statement of fact has been made that is provably false.
- The plaintiff also must prove that the misstatement of fact was the fault of the defendant.
- In addition, if the plaintiff is a "public official" or "public figure," she must prove that the fault amounted to "actual malice," which the court defined as "with knowledge that [the misstatement] was false or with reckless disregard of whether it was false or not."

The basic features of this rule were not new; they had existed in the common law of some states. By giving them constitutional status, *Sullivan* deprived the states of the ability to adjust the playing field at their whim and significantly raised the barrier for most libel plaintiffs. Whether this was an "occasion for dancing in the streets," or a setback for civility, or the sinister entrée for factoid public discourse, or a return to the era of tabloid journalism, is subject to what *Sullivan* hailed as "uninhibited, robust, and wide-open" debate. It is undebatable, however, that Justice William Brennan, the author of *Sullivan,* profoundly changed the legal landscape for all who would participate aggressively in the marketplace of ideas. While the Supreme Court has declined to say whether the rule applies to nonmedia as well as to media defendants, logic and the lower courts generally commend that result, at least where the alleged libel concerns a matter of public interest.

Each aspect of the rule deserves further rumination, but first this caveat: the constitutional defense to a libel action is much more fruitful as a ground for intellectual discussion and legal pan-egyric than it is a productive source of practical guidance for speakers and writers. At the prepublication level, the effect of *Sullivan* is this:

> If you can be sure the subject of your work is a public
> official or public figure, you have more room to mess up.

In court, which is not a place you want to be, *Sullivan* also adds an important, relatively inexpensive (as in the annual wages of only one reporter, not ten) method for disposing of libel suits.

Standard of Care

In 1960, L.B. Sullivan was one of three elected commissioners of the city of Montgomery, Alabama. Among his duties was super-vision of the city's public safety forces. The *New York Times* pub-lished an advertisement paid for by a group of civil rights activists that criticized Montgomery's response to their efforts to gain equal treatment for black citizens. The ad did not identify Sullivan di-rectly, but in his libel suit he claimed that critical references to the Montgomery police were "of and concerning" him. A jury awarded him $500,000 in damages.

Even a passing look at the history of the era makes clear that the real basis for Sullivan's victory was the *New York Times*'s repu-tation for aggressively covering the civil rights struggle. In effect, the libel laws of Alabama were used to punish the *Times* for criti-cizing southern state and local governments.

That the Supreme Court would recognize and correct this ef-fort to revive the Sedition Act was not surprising, but the Court went much further. Not only must citizens be free to criticize gov-ernment and government officials, the Court said, but the "free-doms of expression" must be given "the 'breathing space' that they 'need . . . to survive,' " breathing space that includes the right to be wrong, as well as to be "vehement," "caustic," and "unpleasantly sharp."

Actual Malice

The measure of this "breathing space," as applied to Commissioner Sullivan and other public officials, was to be, in the Court's words, " 'actual malice'—that is, with knowledge that it was false or with reckless disregard of whether it was false or not." The first thing to note about this test is that it has nothing to do with "malice" in the ordinary dictionary sense of "hatred" or "ill will"; the Court might as well have called the test "actual porridge" or "real salmon" for all the use the words are in defining what is meant.

As "actual malice" was defined by the Court, no public official could recover damages without proof that the defendant spoke against him:

- knowing that an allegation was false, or
- recklessly disregarding the allegation's truth.

"Actual malice" was to be the standard of care against which ugly, mean, hurtful, and profoundly damaging speech was to be measured. No matter the harm suffered by a public official, there could be no recovery unless the "actual malice" standard had been breached. Properly applied, the "actual malice" barrier is insurmountable absent misconduct so egregious that it is likely to be found only in the farthest corners of supermarket tabloid exploitation.

Even with the Court's defining words, however, no one can be sure, especially in advance of publication, what "actual malice" is. "Reckless disregard," for example, is particularly unhelpful, because to the ordinary citizen it is too easy to associate with "recklessness" in driving, where there is no deliberate intention to cause harm. Some courts have suggested that a better term would have been "conscious disregard." Perhaps the most useful formulation is one any school child should understand: a knowing lie.

Since *Sullivan,* courts have ruled, sometimes with contradictory results, on hundreds of situations in which a speaker's or writer's conduct has allegedly sunk to the level of "actual malice." Courts have made clear that failure to investigate further, even when other sources are readily available, is not, by itself, conclusive that a writer knew he was uttering falsehoods. However, some cases have held that, when taken with other facts, failure to investigate may be considered by a judge or jury as one component of "actual malice."

Courts also have permitted the following to be used as evidence of "actual malice":

- A history of bad feeling between the parties, in other words, something very like the ill will or spite the dictionary defines as "malice." But, remember, it is not the ill will by itself that matters—a good dose of hatred adds spice to any debate—but the inference of a motive to lie.

- Deliberate alteration of words purportedly spoken by the plaintiff, where "the alteration results in a material change in the meaning conveyed by the statement."

- Reliance on questionable sources, such as anonymous tipsters or persons with a known grudge against the plaintiff, especially when more credible sources are ignored.

- Destruction of notes or other evidence, though this should not be so where the destruction was part of the ordinary course of business unrelated to the potential for a libel claim.

In some ways, the law is more instructive as to what is not "actual malice" than what is. Keep in mind in reviewing the list below that while these were rejected as bases for a finding of "actual malice," they were sufficiently close to have contributed to litigation:

- An "adversarial stance" by the reporter toward the plaintiff
- "Aggressive," "abrasive," or "antagonistic" techniques
- "Vituperation," "exaggerated language," or a "snide or sarcastic tone"
- Failure to interview the plaintiff before publication
- Publication in the face of a denial by the plaintiff

Some factors have been recognized as evidence of *absence* of "actual malice," including:

- Prompt publication of a retraction or correction, though care always must be exercised not to be trapped by a premature, and unnecessary, admission of error
- Reliance on a "variety of mutually corroborative sources and materials"
- Use of an extensive prepublication fact-checking process

"Actual malice" is not the only standard of care to emerge from the reasoning in *Sullivan.* Before the 1970s, in many states, libel was a "strict liability tort." In other words, if you were found to have spoken falsely, it did not matter that you had made an innocent mistake. Thus, if you carefully had taken down facts obtained by phone from the public library, only to find that the librarian had given you erroneous information, you still could be held liable for the resulting damage. A decade after *Sullivan,* in 1974, the Court held that the First Amendment limited nearly all plaintiffs, not just those who were public figures or officials, holding that:

- no one can maintain a libel action without establishing a degree of fault; and
- no one can recover punitive or other damages in excess of "actual injury" without proof of "actual malice."

Damages are one of the great conundrums of libel law. Libel plaintiffs rarely prove actual monetary harm, unlike the victims of personal injury torts, who readily point to medical bills, lost time at work, a missing leg, or a scarred forehead. Unfortunately, the courts do not restrict "actual injury" in libel cases to measurable economic loss. Libel juries may exercise their compassion by awarding huge sums for such murkily quantifiable factors as "impairment of reputation and standing in the community, personal humiliation, and mental anguish and suffering." Raising the "actual malice" barrier to all punitive damages claims restricts the power of juries to get even for decades of real and imagined media slights and newspapers thrown on porch roofs.

Negligence

Requiring some showing of fault from all plaintiffs is better than requiring none, but the threshold of *negligence,* which is the private-figure fault standard adopted in most states, not only is low, it invites a search for the "reasonably prudent journalist." Since journalism, unlike, say, brain surgery, benefits from a certain recklessness on the part of its practitioners, reasonable prudence may not be a positive benefit. Good journalists and public activists are to the casually curious as Indy car drivers are to pleasure motorists.

Negligence is a widely used concept in tort law, generally defined as "lack of ordinary care either in acting or failing to act." Jurors must put themselves in the shoes of the defendant, and decide whether her conduct was the same or better than a mythical "reasonable person." While many states insist that, for libel purposes, the "reasonable person" should not be a professional journalist, the practical effect of the standard is to put the focus on what other journalists or speakers would have done in the same circumstance. Thus, despite statements by some courts that libel should not be an action for journalistic or oratorical malpractice, consciously paying attention to professional standards is a useful approach for writers and speakers in evaluating the culpability of their own conduct.

Any misconduct that equals "actual malice" also will satisfy a negligence standard. In addition, relatively innocent errors that, like excessive speed or insufficiently well-executed left turns for motorists, are part of the everyday lives of writers and speakers may be deemed negligent. Some courts will permit testimony from a journalism professor, or other purported expert, who will explain with great vehemence that no one ever passed his course after betraying such incompetence.

Among the telltale signs of negligence recognized by some courts are:

• Possession in defendant's library of prior reports that are inconsistent with the allegedly libelous version

- Receipt by defendant of information contradicting allegedly libelous version, especially if defendant failed to investigate the conflict

- Reliance on memory absent any effort to check readily available current sources

These examples do not begin to exhaust the list, nor are any of them necessarily conclusive. In each case, there must be evidence, not just that an error occurred, but that reasonable diligence would have avoided it. A finding of negligence is especially dependent on context and judgment and, thus, is much more likely than "actual malice" to be handed over to a jury for ultimate determination.

One clear and important exception to the general rule that any error carries a whiff, if not a presumption, of negligence, is the so-called "wire service defense." A publisher who relies on a known outside source, such as an established wire service, syndicate, or freelance, which has generally proved reliable in the past, can assert successfully that the reliance was reasonable. The publisher is not negligent when he reprints the source's errors. The same rationale should apply to public speakers and writers who openly quote material supplied by others.

Be warned, however, that once you undertake to investigate or rewrite "Doonesbury" or "George Will," or hold yourself out as a proponent of the third party's assertions, the responsibility for the result is your own. Thus in a report on mob influence, it may not be proof against negligence merely to quote another writer's assertion that a waste hauler moonlights as a hit man; if you are expert enough to write about the subject, you are accountable for the reasonableness of your own judgments about the veracity of your material.

Checklist of Care

All of this talk about standards of care is of little practical use to the journalist on deadline or the letter writer about to blow the whistle on the wrongdoer next door. Few set out to knowingly lie, recklessly disregard the truth, or negligently make errors. Only after the deed is done do you look back to wish you had checked an additional fact or more carefully considered your choice of words.

Following this checklist is not a foolproof inoculation against a claim that errors resulted from inexcusable fault, but it is a useful discipline:

- Why is your information credible? Because the source has a prior record of reliability, or has firsthand knowledge? Because the information is consistent with other established facts?

- If the heart of the information is difficult to corroborate, do the lesser details check out? Or are there obvious inconsistencies that should raise doubts? Have you tried to resolve any inconsistencies?

- If you are relying on information contained in documents, have you seen the documents? Do you have copies? Did you work from notes on the documents' contents or only from memory? If you don't have copies, are the originals in a secure place where they will be available to support your interpretation later?

- If you did not see the documents, are you relying on what others told you was in them? Did your sources have access to the documents or were they reporting to you what others have told them?

- If you are relying on what others have told you, are they objective observers? Or do they have a personal stake in publicity for themselves or a motive to injure others? Are they willing to be identified publicly if the facts are challenged?

- Do you know enough to trust your own understanding of what documents say or others have told you? Have you consulted others with greater expertise to assist you?

- Are you confident that documents and other sources present a complete and balanced picture? Is it possible that

other information exists that would change the picture?
What have you done to make sure that you have had access
to all the pieces of the puzzle?

- Have you checked your own files for information that
  might contradict what you are about to say or print? Or
  looked at other obvious sources, like the phone book, that
  are readily at hand?

- Have you made a reasonable effort to give the subjects of a
  negative report an opportunity to comment?

In the hands of good lawyers, the standards of care that flow from
Sullivan have reduced the burden of defending libel suits and en-
couraged potential plaintiffs to heed parental advice about the
proper response to sticks, stones, and names. By exercising care
with their information and thinking ahead about how their work
may be challenged in the harsh gaze of 20/20 hindsight, writers and
speakers can free more lawyers to dance in the streets.

Public Officials, Figures, and Issues

Public figures, as well as public officials, must meet the "actual
malice" burden of proving that speakers of damaging falsehoods
acted with knowledge of falsity or reckless disregard of the truth.
There is no section in the *Yellow Pages* that lists public figures, so,
when you set out to say ugly things about the CEO of a local phone
company, you may not be sure in advance that the courts will insist
that he prove that you knew the ugliness was false before he collects five million dollars.

Even *public official* is not a self-defining term. Elected officials
and law enforcement officers overwhelmingly have been held to
public official status. So have those officials whose appointment
has been subject to a public process—cabinet officials, for example, who must be confirmed by the Congress, or city managers and
school superintendents, who are appointed by a public vote of an
elected body. Schoolteachers and middle- and lower-level bureaucrats are more problematic. The more pervasive the official's pub-

lic power, the less important that the challenged statements be closely tied to the official's public role. The president, for example, or a state governor would be held to public official status even for allegations that in his purely personal capacity he exposed his private anatomy to the maid depositing a mint on the pillow in his vacation hotel room. Traveling down the power scale to, say, a high school social studies teacher, the courts would be more likely to deny public official status unless there is a close nexus between the conduct alleged and the official's public role.

This same nexus between accusation and public role is the touchstone of "public figure" status. A telephone company CEO, unlike a governor, can cavort freely in his vacation hotel room with little risk that comment on his conduct there would be subject to an "actual malice" test. When he is accused of committing the same acts in the boardroom, he risks being held to public figure status. The CEO's status derives from the great power his position enables him to exercise over thousands of employees, millions of customers, and the return to public holders of his company's stock. That power is exercised in the boardroom, and comment related to its exercise logically deserves greater protection than statements about his private life.

The Supreme Court in one brief, glorious moment in the early 1970s offered the promise that anyone whose name appeared in connection with an issue of public importance—in other words, any issue that found its way into the newspaper—would be required to prove that the publisher knew the information was false or recklessly disregarded the truth. The promise evaporated three years later, however, and the test has since been tied to the individual's prominence in attempting to influence a public issue. Ralph Nader or Billy Graham, for example, who hold no public offices, have been so active and so prominent in voicing their views that they should be held to be "pervasive" public figures for purposes of comment on almost any aspect of their lives. Local ministers or public activists who involve themselves in public issues also may be held to be public figures, but only for the narrow purpose of comment on their public roles. An antiabortion activist who speaks out against abortion at rallies, in letters to the editor, and at city council meetings may be a public figure for purposes of a report that she once had an abortion, herself, but she is more likely to be held a private figure if the report is that she is a shoplifter.

For the lawyer defending a libel suit, the distinction between public and private figures is highly significant, since it often makes the difference in convincing a judge to dismiss a libel suit without trial. For the journalist on deadline or the speaker in midsentence on a radio talk show, however, the distinction is seldom of much use. In those relatively few cases where public official or figure status is clear and unquestioned, speakers do have more leeway to speak hastily and journalists may give the benefit of the doubt in quoting detractors of unknown reliability. Most of the time, though, when public status is an open question or an unlikely result, the speaker must presume that she does not have the benefit of the "actual malice" test and look to other means to protect her expression.

Opinion

Traditionally, the term "opinion" had little or no analytical importance to libel law. Then, in 1973, a Supreme Court justice expressed the notion that "there is no such thing as a false idea," leading to a series of lower court decisions—"opinions"?—that gave the term a life of its own. These decisions seemed to hold that a new defense had been created for all expressions that could be construed broadly as opinions, newspaper editorials, for example, or book reviews. Journalists embraced the concept. Skilled defendants' lawyers used it as a shortcut to terminate cases with swift summary judgments. Ultimately, however, this grand new defense foundered on the assertion by a sportswriter that his characterization of a wrestling coach as a liar—a perjurer, in fact, who had lied under oath—was merely an opinion because it had been uttered in a column. When the Supreme Court choked on this extension of the "no such thing as a false idea" doctrine, great wails of pain poured from the ivory towers of editorial writers. They need not have been so chagrined.

The principle remains that a libel plaintiff must prove that a statement of fact has been made about him and that the statement is false. Merely labeling a statement as "opinion" tells nothing about whether it contains a false statement of fact. "In my opinion, I am taller than my brothers," is a statement of fact that easily can be proved, or disproved, with the use of a tape measure. "In my opinion, I am better looking than my brothers," is not a statement of fact because beauty is in the eye of the beholder, not a matter of objective verifiability by commonly accepted standards.

Most editorials and other works of criticism proceed in two steps. First, they state the facts: the actions of the public official, the subject matter of the book, the plot and cast of the play. Then they offer a comment on those facts: "reprehensible," "verbose and humorless," "slow-paced and lackadaisical." When the comments are value judgments, as these are, they are incapable of objective verification, and therefore they cannot be held to be false or true. There is no such thing as a false idea.

If the statements are subject to objective verification—"took the money," "plagiarized the plot," "lied to the court"—it is not a defense merely to proclaim that they appeared in an editorial or review.

FALSE LIGHT AND OTHER TORTS OF QUESTIONABLE ANCESTRY

Other theories of legal liability, besides libel, may find their way into the later paragraphs of the convoluted complaints that creative lawyers waste their formative years learning how to write. The bias of the legal system—and of our civilization—is never to leave an injury uncompensated. A prospective plaintiff with a broken leg does not care what legal theory results in getting his medical bills paid. Torts, such as libel, that have a long history in our jurisprudence also carry much baggage in the form of rules that limit recovery. To get around these rules, and sometimes just to show off their verbal virtuosity, lawyers seldom stop with a simple one-count libel complaint when they can add on counts that purport to derive from other, even more arcane, areas of the law. Most of the time, these creative "two for the price of one" legal theories remain neglected afterthoughts, and lawsuits are resolved on the basic principles of libel. Thanks to the miracle of word processors, lawyers will keep throwing new theories against the wall to see if one sticks.

Some jurisdictions, for example, recognize a tort known as "false light invasion of privacy." Like much else about the law of invasion of privacy, "false light" exists primarily in the minds of law professors. Also, like other aspects of privacy law, it has little or nothing to do with privacy in the ordinary sense of the word. Fortunately, very few false light claims ever have been prosecuted successfully. Only a handful ever have been filed, except as additional claims in libel suits. The only difference between the elements of false light and those of libel is that the falsehood need not be defamatory to be actionable. Thus, in theory, a false statement that would not damage the subject's reputation still may support a lawsuit, if it would cause offense to a person of reasonable sensibilities. In all other respects, the tort of false light should be governed by the same rules as libel.

The two most prominent false light cases involved admittedly fictionalized episodes that purported to describe personal feelings and characteristics of living individuals. The first arose from a play based on the kidnapping of a family and the second from a newspaper feature on the aftermath of a bridge collapse written by a man who wisely abandoned journalism to become one of the highest paid screenwriters in history. Apart from those who write docudramas and, thus, are called upon to create fictional sinews to knot together fragments of reality, most writers and speakers need not lie awake nights fretting over false light claims, unless, of course, they happen to be law professors.

Another favorite theory to add to a libel complaint is a version of intentional or negligent "infliction of emotional distress." Jerry Falwell tacked such a claim onto his libel suit against *Hustler* publisher Larry Flynt, who had the temerity to joshingly portray Mr. Falwell as a man whose "first time" had been with his mother in an outhouse. The jury concluded that Flynt's parody could not be read as a serious assertion of fact, so Falwell's libel claim was, shall we say, tossed in the dumper. The trial court, however, approved a finding that the same facts constituted intentional infliction of emotional distress, a tort that is based on outrageous conduct committed for the purpose of causing psychological harm. The Supreme Court held that this was an impermissible end run around its decision in *New York Times* v. *Sullivan* and reversed Falwell's judgment.

Flynt, by the way, was off on a frolic of his own, suing Falwell for copyright infringement, because Falwell had mailed copies of the parody to millions of potential donors as proof that Satan really was abroad in the world. Flynt, ultimately, was no more successful than Falwell. Of course, the sales of Flynt's magazine didn't suffer, Falwell reaped an untold crop of new contributions and a number of lawyers did quite well on the incident.

At least one state has recognized that a person portrayed unflatteringly may have what amount to contract rights to recover from a publisher. The best known such case involved a newspaper's decision to publish a source's name despite a reporter's promise to protect his identity. The Supreme Court approved a judgment against the newspaper on the theory of "promissory estoppel," holding the newspaper responsible for damage that resulted when the source was fired from his job. Few such claims have been brought, but writers and speakers should resist the temptation to make promises, especially promises of confidentiality, in return for information or cooperation.

Writers and speakers who have a firm grounding in the law of libel and a modicum of common sense need not tie up their brain cells with the details of "promissory estoppel" and "infliction of emotional distress." Just assume that a sufficiently motivated plaintiff always can find some theory to drag you into court. It is, unfortunately, a cost of doing business for those who use words and images, just as any business that uses vehicles can bet that sooner or later one of them will broadside a bus.

II

COMMON LIBEL PROBLEMS

FORGETTING the elements of libel and getting confused about the difference between actual malice and negligence are common and forgivable offenses among journalists and others whose search for truth leaves little time for lawyerly theorizing. This chapter attempts to collect practical warnings and solutions that even sportswriters and talk show hosts easily can comprehend and apply in their own daily chores. Do go back, now and then, and review those basic principles; otherwise, you'll be sorry someday to be maliciously reminded by a private figure plaintiff that your standard of care falls short of the reasonable person's.

CORRECTING ERRORS

The general rule is that publishing a correction does not undo the harm caused by an error, though it may reduce the damages. If you falsely called Smith a thief yesterday and apologized today, most people only thought less of Smith for twenty-four hours, though a few may never catch up to the truth. Perhaps, instead of $1 million, you owe Smith $100,000; the jury will take the correction into account in deciding how much you have to pay. The dilemma is this: while there is no way to be sure how impressed the jury will be with your forthrightness and generosity in correcting an error until their verdict is returned, correcting an error conclusively establishes that you made one.

Many states have addressed this problem by passing statutes that enhance the effect of a timely retraction. "Retraction statutes" vary widely in their terms, which may be quite technical and apply only to a narrow range of specific media, not to all speakers. The best of them, like California's, are immensely valuable to publishers who can qualify for their protection. To recover most types of libel damages from California newspapers and broadcasters (the statute, unfortunately, may not apply to magazines, books, pamphleteers, soapbox speakers, and others), the prospective plaintiff must demand a correction in writing from the publisher within twenty days after learning of publication. If a correction is published, in substantially as prominent a position as the error, within twenty-one days after receipt of the demand, the plaintiff can collect no more than "special damages," which are narrowly defined in the statute to mean only actual out-of-pocket losses.

Writers and speakers should be aware of their state's specific rules on retractions, but some principles apply everywhere. The first is to take seriously any suggestion of error and react to it with the same degree of professionalism you would expect to receive when returning a defective shoe to Nordstrom or Nieman-Marcus. A few news organizations assign a specific individual, often called an ombudsman or readers' representative, to accept calls and letters of complaint. This means that complaints are reviewed by someone more objective than the writer or editor accused of the error. Most complaints have nothing to do with legal liability, since most purported errors do not present the elements of libel or any other tort, and a knowledgeable ombudsman or editor usually can tell when a complaint presents a legal threat.

Do not react to any complaint, especially one involving legal concerns, with a confession of error or implied criticism of the perpetrating writer or editor. Whatever you say to the complainant is, like the "Oh-my-god-I'm-sorry!" at the scene of an accident, admissible as evidence. The same is true of an aggressively offensive defensiveness, like "What's a matter with you! You bleeping idiot!"

Equally damaging, if the plaintiff is smart enough to discover them, are internal discussions about the ancestry of either the reporter or the complainant, especially memos written to assign blame. Investigate accusations of serious error carefully and thoroughly, but with a degree of circumspection and objectivity that will lead to a sound assessment of the truth, rather than a botched attempt at redirecting blame. Involving a lawyer in the investigation is wise, both because the decision to retract may require legal judgments and the documents and discussions generated in a legal investigation may be privileged from disclosure to the other side.

News organizations in the past erred in the direction of being too resistant to correcting their mistakes. If anything, the pendulum has swung in the opposite direction, especially among newspapers, which seem almost to revel in confessing error, like so many reformed spousal abusers on the "Oprah" show. Do not be too quick to jump to the conclusion that you were wrong. Once you are sure, the best response usually is a full, clear, unequivocal correction. Even if such a correction does not immunize you from suit, or deter the plaintiff, it will enhance your position with both judge and jury and make it more likely that you will get the benefit of the many legal barriers that plaintiffs must hurdle.

A good correction makes clear that an error was made. "We *incorrectly* said Jones steals; in fact, he's an attorney" is better than "We said Jones steals; he's an attorney."

A good correction makes clear what the error was. "We incorrectly said Jones is an ax-murderer; in fact, he's an accountant" is better than, "We incorrectly identified Jones's profession; he's a bookkeeper." (Note that in some states, plaintiffs still can find cases that support the twisted notion that repeating the error in the correction constitutes a second libel and aggravates the damages.)

A good correction is displayed as prominently, sometimes more prominently, than the error. Many newspapers handle this by running corrections in a standard position on page two or three. Occasionally, however, a potentially libelous error is on page one, or in a headline in large type. On such occasions, it may be best to put the correction on page one or in large type, as well. The key is to display the correction so that those who would have noticed the error are at least as likely to notice the correction. If there is a retraction statute in your state, it may be especially important to publish the correction in the same location as the error.

A little humility is good for everyone, but it is not a legal requirement. Thus, it isn't necessary to "regret" errors or "apologize" for them. Do make sure that complaints get routed promptly to someone who can respond to them politely and authoritatively. An answering machine with a solid-sounding greeting is better than a live nineteen-year-old news clerk chewing gum.

Surprisingly, many who make their livelihoods describing events in print or in the visual media are as awestruck as the hapless witness to a car wreck to learn that there is more than one way to view or describe an event. The professionals are so conditioned to avoid error that they honestly are astonished when accused of committing one. Especially flabbergasting is the assumption, whether by outraged plaintiff or indignant editor, that a newspaper, which publishes millions of facts each year, should not get a few hundred wrong.

PREPUBLICATION CHECKLIST

The following section aims to anticipate the aggravations of dealing with lawyers in an arcane practice known as "prepublication review," or, more colloquially, "vetting." The examples reflect common problems found in journalism, but they have counterparts in other forms of writing and speaking.

SOURCES. Far too many reporters and not a few editors still believe that no report is good without an occasional attribution to "sources." Whenever the word finds its way into a report (unless it is something so innocuous as, "Sources said the average annual precipitation in Buenos Aires is 37.4 inches"), consider carefully the terms of the source relationship. What kind of anonymity was promised? In most cases, no specific promises were made. The reporter has chosen to attribute to "sources" because he is too lazy to explain who the source is or because he has a vague sense that leaving out the name will enhance his relationship with the source. In such cases, follow one of three courses:

- Identify the source
- Eliminate the attribution altogether
- Go back to the source before publication and make sure the source agrees that the reporter will be free to identify the source if the report is questioned

In those few cases where there is a clear understanding that the source is never to be revealed and where the information obtained from the source is crucial to the report and unavailable from any other source, significant risk results. If the report is challenged, it will be extremely difficult to defend.

PROMISES, PROMISES. While you are straightening out your relationships with sources, keep in mind that courts may deem off-hand and ill-considered comments to be binding contracts. Do not make promises to sources, especially promises about protecting identity, if you, or your editors, do not intend to abide by them. An oral contract is no less binding than one that is signed, sealed, and delivered, and breaching it is a sure route to a lawsuit.

SHODDY EDITING. A well-edited news report very seldom needs help from a lawyer. If the editor is first-rate, about all he will need to know from a lawyer is how to move just a little bit closer to the edge of the precipice without tumbling into the hole. Unsurprisingly, however, not all editors are first-rate, and many of the best ones have an occasional off day. Lack of clarity, disorganization, internal inconsistencies, poor research, unnecessary ambiguity, anything that clouds a report's meaning all lead to potential legal disputes besides damaging the quality of communication.

ABSENT ATTRIBUTION. A report that "Aunt Toots *says* Uncle Clyde is a bad shot," is different than "Uncle Clyde *is* a bad shot." While laying the blame for a damaging statement on someone else is not a complete defense to a libel claim, avoid converting bald assertions into statements of fact. Feature writers, especially, hate to burden their work with "he saids" and "she saids." Thus, they write, "Poor Ms. Green was beaten by her former husband," when the only evidence is what Ms. Green told them. Just adding an attribution may not protect you from Mr. Green's wrath, but leaving it out makes your lawyer's job more difficult and misleads your readers about the state of the evidence.

FAMILY FEUDS. Speaking of Aunt Toots, her estimate of your capacity for alcohol or your propensity to kick the dog is no more reliable than the average soothsayer's. Nevertheless, reporters' otherwise finely tuned senses of disbelief often turn to tin when the accuser is a family member, or, especially, a former family member. Be as wary of assertions by a spouse or other relative as you would be about a politician's claims about his opponent.

GRATUITOUS JABS. Malicious intent aside, reporters frequently lack what might be called a feeling of conviviality toward the people they write about. "Greaseball," "sleazebag," "lower than pond scum," and "scam artist" usually do not find their way into print, but they occasionally slip into the argot of American newsrooms. Such words also capture in more graphic terms the feelings, usually fully justified, that reporters attempt to convey with more subtlety in their reports. Thus, in a report about difficulties at a financial institution—difficulties unrelated to any provable wrongdoing —reporters betray their true feelings about the institution's officers by alluding to such extraneous details as the oil stains on the parking lot or the heavy beard of the institution's president. These colorful details probably are not defamatory, but they often lend to a report the atmosphere of skullduggery that pushes the subject far enough over the edge to resort to a lawsuit. Examine such details closely and eliminate those that do not advance the story.

EXTRANEOUS NAMES. Names make news, someone said, and many reporters and editors feel they are enhancing their service to readers by loading reports with as many names as possible. Where such practices merely lead to extended lists of pallbearers at funerals, they raise few legal concerns. However, in reports about wrongdoing and shady business dealing, the fewer names in the report the better, at least from the libel lawyer's perspective. Whenever there is any doubt, always ask if particular names are important enough to remain in the report. Ask the same question about faces that appear in the background of photographs—a tighter crop not only makes for greater graphic impact, it may avoid a needless legal squabble with an innocent bystander.

SLOPPILY SCORED SUBMELODIES. As with names, there are many degrees of importance in the components of a report, especially a long one. Libel suits are as apt to be triggered by an obscure reference in the thirty-seventh paragraph as by the main points in the lead. Not only has the libel lawyer lost interest by the thirty-seventh paragraph, the editor and reporter may have as well. One more reason, apart from protecting spotted owl habitat, why long reports are of questionable utility. Make sure the minor themes in a report are as well supported as the arias.

HEADLINES, CUTLINES, AND OTHER SHORTCUTS TO COURT. The headlines and cutlines are written by copy editors who may be blissfully ignorant of all the care the reporter took to avoid legal problems. A copy editor at *Barron's* once inscribed beneath a lawyer's photograph the caption, "Sinatra's mouthpiece." The lawyer managed to keep *Barron's* publisher Dow Jones in court for several years before reason prevailed. Headline and caption writers have one primary goal: make the product fit the space assigned. The headline size and style assignment cannot be changed because the report is too complicated to describe in eighteen letters. As a result, headline writers are tempted to change the report instead. "Stock scam" fits better than "securities irregularities." Take as much care with the headline and other aspects of the visual presentation of information as you do with the text. Copy editors have an uncanny way of making a headline say in seventy-two-point type what the reporter worked for hours to avoid saying in the text.

TAKE-OUT QUOTES. A common feature of newspaper and magazine makeup is the "take-out quote." That's when the juiciest line in the article is excerpted, set in larger type, and used as a graphic element on the page. Statements that look fair and balanced in context in ten-point type somehow become glaringly unsettling when pulled out of context and set in thirty-six-point type. Make sure someone looks closely at the finished page proof (or the broadcaster's final cut) on especially sensitive reports.

STICKY PICTURES. Photos are not likely to lead to libel problems, unless subjected to digital trickery or combined with misleading words. Photos often are miscaptioned, however, and the innocent victim's name may appear in type under the perpetrator's picture. Also, the use of photos and other graphic elements can put a different light on the accompanying text. Another reason to examine the finished page proof with care.

LEADING QUESTIONS. Questions may be inquiries in search of answers, or they may be another way of stating an answer, as in the caption, "Another Hitler?" The use of questions in headlines and captions is a common shortcut, usually frowned upon by editing mavens. Rhetorical questions also are a staple of political debate. If the purpose of the question is to assert the answer, a court may construe it as such.

PROMOTIONS. Promotional spots and lead-in language in broadcasting, as well as rack cards and other print promotion gimmicks, are used to build interest in sensitive, carefully lawyered stories. Too often, unfortunately, no one lawyers the promotion department. Try to anticipate these shots to the foot before they are fired.

STOCK FOOTAGE. Broadcasters must have engaging film and graphics regardless of their relation to the report in question. Print media, too, may pull stock material out of the file to illustrate a report. Try not to use shots of celebrity fashion shows to illustrate reports about streetwalkers. It upsets the streetwalkers.

BROAD GENERALIZATIONS. A study commissioned several decades ago urged reporters and editors not to be content with reporting the facts, but to try to report the "truth about the facts." This is a worthy platitude. However, reporters make trouble for themselves when they refuse to let the facts speak for themselves and draw the conclusions from those facts that all know are warranted but none can prove.

SNEAKY TRANSITIONS. Writers like their work to flow. "Make it sing," is a common newsroom exhortation. Often a "trend" report will bring together examples of loosely related but very different activities. Thus, a report on real estate sales practices may discuss a number of new wrinkles, some of them clearly legal and aboveboard, others much less so. Reporters try to weave the different examples together, comparing and contrasting with plenty of "on the one hand" and "on the other hand" language. The danger is that clean practices will get closely intertwined with not-so-clean practices and not-so-clean practices will find themselves closely compared to the clearly dirty. Make sure reports are worded precisely and say exactly what they mean and no more.

TONE. Never forget that at trial, the plaintiff's lawyer will try to display a huge blowup of either (a) the one sentence you messed up on; or (b) if, as is more likely, you carefully saw to the sanctity of each sentence, the entire report. In the latter case, the argument will be that any ordinary reader would understand that such a report would not have been written except as part of a calculated campaign to unfairly damage and destroy the poor plaintiff, who admittedly is culpable of each charge alleged, but does not deserve to be cast in such a negative light. Never mind that a good judge would not let a case go to trial on such a theory (there is a limited supply of good judges), you cannot ignore the overall tone of the work.

TRUTH. On the state of today's law, it is hard to be sure that there is ever such a thing as a libel-proof plaintiff. Still, certain classes of hominids seem to be harder to libel than others: mobsters, sports stars, and presidential candidates come to mind (that's why there's nothing scarier to a libel lawyer than hearing that a longtime sports, political, or mob reporter has been assigned to cover the aerospace business). The last line of defense—and to some degree, the first line—is that a report is true. All libel lawyers savor the thought of a jury's judgment of truth on all counts (almost as much as they savor the enormous fees they will earn getting there). All libel lawyers also know that the real value of truth as a defense is in the calculation that guilty potential plaintiffs must make about the risk of a trial. John Gotti has too many other pressing litigation problems to be fooling around with a libel suit. Many statements that otherwise would be foolish to print are relatively risk-free if the reporter and his editors are sure, very sure, that the facts are right. It is also important to make sure, very sure, that the reporter and his editors know the consequences if the facts are wrong.

INARTFUL TERMS. Journalists and others whose goal in using words is to be understood by general audiences, not to prove membership in a secret society, strive for "plain meaning." Every trade, however, seems to have its own dictionary, in which shovels are "utilitarian earth-moving implements." Most of the time, good communication—and clear thinking—is best advanced by calling a shovel a shovel. Occasionally, however, precision requires respect for the special definitions conferred on a profession's "terms of art." A "charge," for example, has a specific meaning in criminal jurisprudence that is more narrow than the plain English definition. Many libel suits result from the failure to use such terms precisely.

THE SOILED NEST. Extraneous thoughts sometimes stain reporters' note pads: "the lying son of a bitch" may be scrawled in the margin of notes on the interview with a major source. Look closely at documents and notes to make sure that the well isn't poisoned. Reporters and editors seldom understand the degree to which the entire editorial process will be scrutinized if the case is litigated vigorously. Only a handful are sued, and those who have been subjected to skillfully prosecuted lawsuits are very rare indeed. Thus, they often do not recognize just how damaging the loss of key notes (or even the failure to write legibly) or extraneous misbehavior in the news-gathering process damages their ultimate chances of success. Libel verdicts are largely a question of which side the jury likes least, and there are things that happen in reporting that juries will hate. Do what you can before publication to make sure you look as warm and cuddly as possible.

OTHER PEOPLE'S LAWSUITS. Always try to anticipate how a report might become part of somebody else's law suit. Investigative reports about public disputes often lead to litigation between the principals. If you can figure out where these lawsuits are likely to come from, you can find ways to minimize your exposure to a subpoena. For example, it sometimes is a good idea to add a little extra information to a report so it is clear from the face of it where to find the other witnesses who could corroborate it. Other times, you may want to adhere with extra care to your established practice concerning the preservation of notes and other materials or the return of documents to their sources.

CARRY OUT THE TRASH. Do follow a consistent practice in retaining notes and other documentation, including computer files. Consistent practices may range from keeping nothing to keeping everything. You do not want to pull a Rose Mary Woods: "Yes, your honor, my client has everything except this one page in his notes on his crucial interview with the now deceased percipient witness, half of which seems to have disappeared somewhere. He thinks he might have torn it off to wrap some used chewing gum."

DOCUMENTATION AND SOURCES

Two points, the first and the last, in the preceding checklist deserve extra attention. Why is it that reliance on unnamed sources bedevils the defense of a libel suit? And, who is Rose Mary Woods and how do we avoid her problem?

Rose Mary Woods was Richard Nixon's secretary; she got the blame for the crucial gap in one of Nixon's more incriminating office tape recordings. Possibly, Nixon could have salvaged his career had the tape gap not reinforced the view that he was leading a cover-up. Possibly not.

Anyone facing the prospect of litigation must prepare to have the most intimate details of life put under a microscope, especially those details that relate directly to the alleged wrongful act. Home telephone records may be subpoenaed as well as records of airlines, credit card, car rental, and hotel companies that could shed light on the writer's movements and personal contacts. Once the lawsuit is filed, both parties lose much of their flexibility to attend to those New Year's resolutions about cleaning the desk or making a planned run to the Salvation Army. After you're hit by the truck, it is too late to change out of that stained underwear before the doctor starts probing.

To be prepared, have a regular practice of handling notes, documents, and drafts, including those stored in computers or other media. Do not assume that computer files you thought you had erased also are gone from a system manager's backup tape or that coworkers are as orderly as you in eliminating carbon copies of memos and drafts. The details of your practice are less important than that it be followed religiously. One not entirely facetious approach is to keep a box at the end of your desk. On the first of the month, put everything from your desk into the box. During the following month, retrieve anything you need out of the box and put it back on your desk. When the month ends, throw everything that's still in the box into the trash and start over. Repeat the process monthly. If you are ever in Miss Woods's position, you should have little or no difficulty explaining what happened to the missing excerpt.

Most journalists assume that it is better to keep too much documentation than too little. Lawyers divide on the question. Those who prefer packrats believe that copies of notes, tape recordings, or research materials will help establish that news reports were written carefully and statements accurately quoted. Those in the Dumpster school—including the present author—believe that the report itself is the best evidence of what the reporter knew at the time it was written. Notes, and especially early drafts, do little other than open a foggy window into the sausage factory. Dumpsterites urge reporters to regularly (weekly is fine; daily is better) dispose of notes and other materials, unless they relate to a continuing project and will be needed again soon. If it is important to keep material, then it is also important to devote the time necessary to make sure that old notes are legible and organized and that files are orderly and readily retrievable. Given a choice between using a wastebasket and spending time on what they regard as clerical chores, most reporters opt for the trash.

Unnamed sources, just like notepads with missing pages, give fits to libel defendants. The ultimate issue in modern libel suits often is whether the writer or speaker behaved reasonably in choosing to rely on a source for the accuracy of information. The reasonableness of conduct is the touchstone of "negligence," the minimum standard of care applicable to most libel suits. Establishing that it was reasonable to rely on a source who cannot be identified is a neat trick. Even establishing that the reporter is not knowingly lying may be impossible if a court rules that a jury should presume that sources without names do not exist. It does not matter how many unnamed sources a reporter has, if she cannot name them, she cannot establish that she was reasonable in relying on them or that she believed what the sources told her.

Shield laws—statutes that limit a reporter's duty to testify—typically do not apply when the reporter is a defendant. Instead of ordering the reporter to divulge the source, the judge may put him to the Hobson's choice of naming the source or accepting a ruling that the sources do not exist. In sum, defamatory statements attributable only to anonymous sources are ticking time bombs tied to the writer's breast. Avoid them or reach an understanding with the source that her identity can be revealed if a suit is filed.

III

PRIVATE FACTS

NO ASPECT OF THE LAW affecting expression is more fraught with evil potential than the law of invasion of privacy. "Privacy" has become a twentieth-century idol. Like many idols, however, privacy means many different things to different people in different contexts.

The particular permutation of privacy that jabs journalists most sharply is the purported right to use the courts to obtain multimillion-dollar judgments from defendants who have done nothing more than publish the truth. This is a variety of invasion of privacy known as public disclosure of private facts. It is one of four separate "privacy" torts described by a distinguished professor of tort law, whose work in the area is widely accepted as the basis for state interpretations. The professor divided invasion of privacy claims into four categories: (1) public disclosure of private facts, (2) intrusion, (3) commercial appropriation, and (4) false light.

False light is almost indistinguishable from libel and is discussed in the chapter on libel. Pure false light claims are very rare. *Commercial appropriation* claims are closely akin to copyright and other claims arising out of information property rights, and are discussed in the chapter on property rights. *Intrusion* is hard to distinguish from trespass, the ancient common law right to protect property from uninvited interlopers. Unlike the other categories, the cause of action is unrelated to publication. Intrusion and trespass are discussed in the chapter on news-gathering fouls.

Unlike libel, *public disclosure of private facts* presumes that the information published is true. Unlike intrusion or trespass, it has nothing to do, at least in theory, with the manner in which the information is obtained. And unlike commercial appropriation, there

46

need be no allegation that the information was used for commercial gain. Thus, this theory might be applied to frame a cause of action against a photographer who openly takes a picture in a nondistorting manner of a public event or a reporter who accurately copies information from a police report.

Fortunately, the specter of the "private facts" tort has initiated more law review articles by professors and spirited discussion among the media and their lawyers than it has actual lawsuits. This is partly because one of the elements of the tort is lack of public interest in the facts disclosed. Most published facts and photographs are almost by definition "newsworthy," at least in the minds of editors and publishers.

The other key element of private facts is that the facts disclosed must be highly offensive to persons of ordinary sensibilities. While a few courts have suggested that some facts may be so outrageously offensive as to overwhelm any claim that they are nevertheless newsworthy, plaintiffs generally must prove both offensiveness and want of public interest.

A series of Supreme Court decisions concerning the right to publish information from the public record—the names of rape victims, for example, and the identities of youthful offenders—has added a constitutional dimension to the private-facts tort. The Supreme Court cases appear to stand for the right to publish anything lawfully obtained from public records, particularly court records, no matter how offensive or lacking in public interest the facts may be. These cases stop short, however, of declaring absolute protection, and plaintiffs can be counted on to continue to press for ways around them.

Defense counsel always can find a way to argue, with more than mock sincerity, that almost anything published that is truthful is also legal. Publishers can save legal fees and still publish most of the news if common sense and care are exercised. Some situations that should be approached with special caution:

OLD FELONIES. Many private-facts claims have resulted from the resurrection of old information about criminals who have since reformed. One of the earliest successful plaintiffs was a retired prostitute whose former life was made into a movie, *The Red Kimono,* without her consent some years after she had settled into life as an inconspicuous housewife. The constitutional decisions immunizing the accurate reporting of information lawfully obtained from public records should make cases like this impossible for plaintiffs to win today, at least under the rubric of the private-facts tort.

FADED GLORY. Others, whose fifteen minutes of fame involved no felonies but nevertheless have long since ebbed, seem particularly testy about being dragged back into the limelight. One early plaintiff had been a notorious child prodigy whose life as an adult recluse was interrupted by a *New Yorker* profile. This case, too, would be unlikely to result today in a victory for the plaintiff, but any use of old news, especially old news about people unconnected to current events, should send off alarm bells and receive careful consideration before publication.

MEDICAL DETAILS. An accurate report that a person suffers from a devastating disease, cancer or AIDS, for example, should not be so offensive as to be deemed a private fact, but reporting the details of medical problems often stirs sensitive reactions, especially if it is done gratuitously. Thus, identifying an otherwise nonnewsworthy victim, without his permission, in a feature story on the effects of AIDS, may be to court unnecessary trouble.

GRIEF. The mythical image of the reporter thrusting a microphone in the face of the grieving widow at the scene of the homicide is a favorite of politicians and others seeking to make points at the expense of the press. That it seldom happens, or, when it does, that the widow herself may be eager to vent her feelings, seems irrelevant to most press critics. Still, the appeal of the image to the average citizen, including those who sit on juries or as judges, seems undeniable. Be careful when depicting scenes of grief or other intense personal emotion.

RIDICULE. Depicting otherwise public facts in intentionally, or unintentionally, deprecating ways should be approached with caution. Elderly people in exercise classes seem to have a special distaste for publicity, as does anyone whose portliness, mussed hair, disarrayed clothing, or other characteristics are portrayed for no other apparent purpose than the amusement of others. When such portrayals are based on public observations, they should not present legal problems, but when obtained surreptitiously, retrieved from old or nonpublic sources, or used in ways that differ from the purpose that led to their creation, hazards loom.

ENDANGERMENT. Courts are especially solicitous of plaintiffs who can argue that publication caused a danger of physical retaliation. One plaintiff convinced a court that publishing her name in an article about the death of her roommate unreasonably exposed her to a risk that the murderer might retaliate against her. The case was made more difficult because the defendant was unable to establish with certainty that the name was obtained from public records.

INNOCENT BYSTANDERS. A number of successful private-facts claims have been brought by relatives or associates of those whose notoriety is unquestioned, including, for example, Betty Friedan's former husband, the wife of Ernest Hemingway, and the children of the Rosenberg spies. In each case, the relatives or associates were able to show that the newsworthiness of others did not rub off on them. These cases should be read as a caution to make sure that independent acts, not just accidents of genealogy, warrant including the names of bit players.

Photographers are at special risk of private-facts claims, because the normally helpful presumption that a photograph proves itself, merely establishes the offense. The potential of a private-facts lawsuit means photographers must be very careful in shooting:

- Scenes of "private" emotion, grief being the most obvious example

- In nonpublic places, hospital rooms, for example, without creating a record that they were there with permission

- In ways that reveal in an offensive way personal characteristics, such as unusual physical features or disabilities

None of this means that such pictures shouldn't be taken, only that sensitivity and care should be exercised, both in the shots selected and in the photographer's conduct in taking them. Though the outrageousness of the photo's use, not of the photographer's demeanor, should be the touchstone of private-facts liability, judges and juries will not ignore egregious conduct.

IV

NEWS-GATHERING FOULS

A LL TWO YEAR OLDS discover that shooting off the mouth can trigger a backlash. Toddlers also learn that, even with lips zipped, poking around in other people's business can lead to unfortunate consequences. While libel law is the dominant substitute for hickory switches on adults who speak too freely, other remedies apply to those who silently pry. Among the more common are the old-fashioned tort of trespass, the newer-fangled variety of privacy invasion known as intrusion, and, for those who stumble into the hands of cranky cops, criminal charges for obstructing justice. Seldom are any of these pursued to ultimate judgment against reporters and others whose only goal is information to be shared publicly, but they can serve as powerful weapons to deter unwary truth seekers.

Even with the truth safely in hand, potential speakers and writers may run afoul of lawyers seeking to invoke the power of the courts to block dissemination of information by using an ancient cudgel known as prior restraint.

TRESPASS

The most hallowed tradition of the law is the protection of private property. Venture uninvited across the threshold of another and risk a perfectly legal horsewhipping or garroting. The privileges of private property include the right to deny access to reporters, as well as to Bonnie and Clyde.

Trespass is a strict liability tort; if you are on the property of another without permission or excuse, even if by accident or mistake, you are liable. Fortunately, unlike libel, damages for trespass are narrowly limited, which means that, apart from the cost of replacing your divots, you probably aren't liable for enough to make it worth the owner's while to sue you. That's why very few trespass actions have been brought against reporters or others seeking information for lawful purposes.

The threat of a trespass action, however, particularly for the harm it will do to a reporter's credibility, as well as for the license it gives the property owner and her dogs to have their way with him, can be a serious impediment to truth seeking. Thus, it is helpful to know these limits of trespass law:

- So long as permission, implied or express, is obtained, it is perfectly proper to visit another's property. The presence of a doorbell button is an invitation to ring it and to go inside if a person who appears to be in charge invites you, even if the invitation is later rescinded.

- An invitation to enter may be implied by the nature of the premises. Restaurateurs, for example, usually do not expect their patrons to ask permission to cross the threshold. An invitation also may be implied from past practice. If property is routinely used as a gathering place without objection from the owner, a roving information seeker is at little risk by joining the party.

- Invitations may be revoked or limited. When told to depart by someone with apparent authority who speaks firmly, be prepared to leave by the most direct route available. If you are told not to use your camera or tape recorder, or to stay out of the back room, those limitations are enforceable. They also are subject to change at the whim of the owner.

- An implied invitation to enter a restaurant to dine or a mortuary to mourn does not necessarily imply an invitation to take pictures or make speeches.

- Because trespass is an offense against possession, only the owner, tenant, or someone acting with the owner's authority has the right to deny access; your fellow mourners can throw you out bodily, but only the mortician and his deputies have the right to assert the law of trespass against you.

- While public property is exempt from the laws of trespass, the state can invoke its other powers to deny access for purposes that it deems inconsistent with the normal use of the property. (See the discussion of public places in the "Access" chapter.)

- While private owners of property not normally open to the public can deny access on whatever basis catches their fancy, including distaste for something said about them in last week's *Bugle,* the keepers of public property may not discriminate against someone for exercising First Amendment rights.

- Increasingly, malls and other private facilities have taken over the social role formerly played by public squares and sidewalks, and the owners' power to foreclose use of such facilities for traditional First Amendment purposes, including speaking and leaflet distributing, has become more circumscribed.

- Trespass laws extend only to access to the property itself, not the right to listen to or view events or conditions from outside the premises or even to overfly the premises.

- When public authorities take possession of a scene of crime or disaster, they may act in the owner's place to grant or deny access. Mere presence of public authorities, however, and their acquiescence in a reporter's joining them does not override the owner's rights. When the owners of a private residence summon paramedics to assist a heart attack victim, they may not anticipate that an Eyewitness News camera will come in along with the defibrillator.

- Obtaining entry by false pretenses may render the whole visit a trespass.

When in doubt, ordinary citizens are best advised to err in favor of not committing a trespass. Reporters and others attempting to enlighten the public sometimes must push the edge of the envelope.

INTRUSION

An action for the variety of invasion of privacy known as intrusion offers two potential advantages to plaintiffs over an action for trespass:

- The rules on recovery of damages are more liberal
- While it usually involves some type of entry onto private real property, an intrusion can occur in an otherwise public place, or on someone's property other than the victim's

Until recently, few intrusion cases have been litigated successfully, and the damages awarded have been nominal. The rise of so-called "reality" programs on television seems to have put a premium on extended recording of stressful encounters between citizens and public authorities. One byproduct of this trend has been an upsurge of intrusion claims, or, at least, greater news media concern about them.

As defined in the cases that have been litigated, as well as in many pounds of professorial maundering, the tort of intrusion is an intentional act that intrudes on someone's private affairs in a highly offensive way. In theory, dissemination of information obtained in an act of intrusion is irrelevant to the questions of whether a tort occurred or what damages should be due. Nevertheless, juries cannot help but be affected by evidence that the information obtained in the course of the claimed intrusion has been widely disseminated.

The same rules that apply to trespass will help avoid intrusion claims. Some additional cautions:

- Surreptitious conduct, especially involving listening devices, long lenses, or other James Bond–like techniques, should be undertaken, if at all, with special care.

- Harassing behavior, of the sort favored by paparazzi-style photographers, will make news gathering, even that which occurs in an obviously public place, more vulnerable to an intrusion claim.

- Even if public authorities appear to encourage your presence and the use of cameras and recorders at scenes of crisis, make sure that permission is clear and, if possible, recorded on the tape or film.

- Exercise careful judgment in selecting and displaying photographs and other material obtained surreptitiously, by surprise, or in other ways that juries might find oppressive or unfair.

- Be especially careful about using such film or tape for promotional purposes or as stock footage to illustrate unrelated incidents.

Remember, finally, some of the best journalism and some of the most acute attacks in public debate derive from tactics that might make Miss Manners cringe. So it goes. But do not undermine good information with unnecessarily bizarre or oppressive conduct.

CROSSING POLICE AND THEIR LINES

Police have guns, nightsticks, handcuffs, and tear gas. It usually is not a good idea to argue too vehemently with them, or to blithely step over that yellow tape they string around places they do not want the rest of us to be. In some states the news media are entitled to statutory exemptions from the general authority of the police to cordon off areas, but even these are of no great help in the face of itchy nightsticks.

Nevertheless, journalists and others with a legitimate interest in police activities usually are given reasonable access. Some tips for making sure that is the case:

- Generally, good relations with local police are a product of hard work over a long period of time, not First Amendment fulmination at the scene of the crime. News organizations should make police-press relations a priority and develop connections at the highest levels. Pledges of fealty to First Amendment values extracted over lunch are awkward, though not impossible, to retract over the tensions of a hostage situation.

- Local police agencies often issue credentials to journalists; most of the time, though, such credentials are more of a convenience than a requirement. When news breaks and the dog has eaten your pass, if you look professional and carry a notepad, most police agencies won't question your status.

- The police, like other government officials, cannot lawfully confer or deny benefits based on the exercise of First Amendment rights; thus, the *Bugle*'s press passes should not be yanked because the sheriff was not endorsed for reelection.

- Cranky cops sometimes arrest journalists and attempt to confiscate notes or film. Even though they may know the arrests will not stand up, their immediate goal of removing an irritant will have been met. There is no surefire protection in such circumstances. The best tactics are Ghandi's, not Casey Stengel's: Hold your temper; do nothing to provoke retaliation; speak softly but firmly, making clear your disagreement; follow clear orders; do not resist; keep taking notes or making pictures until told to stop; get word of your predicament to your superiors, or your lawyer. Above all else, get the attention of higher ranking officers as soon as possible; lieutenants and captains are much more sensitive to the long-range consequences of shackling journalists than the average cop on the beat.

- Publicize problems. Law enforcement agencies are political entities. Let readers and viewers know when police are denying information the public should know. Just be careful not to make yourself look like an arrogant, spoiled child while you're doing it.

If an arrest sticks and politics and common sense do not prevail, the risk of a journalist's facing conviction for criminally interfering with a police officer is very real. The First Amendment offers few arguments for immunity from prosecution unless there is evidence of discriminatory treatment or a motive to retaliate for what was published.

ELECTRONIC EAVESDROPPING

There are stringent federal laws against wiretapping, electronically gaining access to telephone communications without the knowledge of the participants in the call. In addition, some states have statutes that make it a crime for one participant in a private conversation, including a phone conversation, to record it without the permission of all other participants. These laws may reflect profound public fears about the magical powers of electronic instruments, much as many primitive societies have taboos against photography. Whatever their origin, however, such laws must be taken seriously if journalists and other truth seekers are to avoid the horrible dilemma that results from having the goods on the bad guys but being unable to publish without facing a jail term.

None of these laws forbid overhearing things that are supposed to be private; they only apply to the use of electronic listening and recording devices, including extension phones, and, in some cases, cellular telephone monitoring devices. So, if the bad guys do their plotting at the next table and you overhear them and take good notes, fine. Be careful, however, about hiding the tape recorder in the flowers or using directional mikes. Also, if you do plan to record, it usually is best to announce your intention to do so on the tape so no one can argue they were surreptitiously recorded.

An aside about the value of tape recordings: The hubris that attends righteousness sometimes leads reporters to believe that if the jurors hear the tape, they will conclude inevitably that the bad guy had it coming. Sometimes, unfortunately, especially when coached by a skilled plaintiff's attorney, the jurors are just as likely to conclude that the reporter was arrogant, unprofessional, and reckless with the truth. Tapes are expensive; it is a good idea to recycle them.

WORKING UNDERCOVER

Most journalism and other fact-gathering activities are best done openly and obviously. However, misrepresentation by a journalist or other citizen in search of information is not necessarily illegal and sometimes may be the only way to get the job done. Restaurant reviewers, for example, do their work best when the maître d' is deceived about their status. Much consumer reporting can only succeed if auto mechanics or other service providers are blithely ignorant that an apparently hapless customer is a reporter. If you are contemplating working undercover, keep these points in mind:

- It is one thing to allow someone to assume what he wants about you; it is something else to lie.
- Using electronic or other James Bond–style gadgets is more difficult to defend then skulking about or simple failure to identify yourself.
- Failure to clearly identify yourself as a journalist or otherwise accurately state your purpose is more likely to present legal problems if the target is unsophisticated or underage.

Always weigh carefully whether the information sought can be obtained in a more open way, or, if not, whether its value to your audience justifies the potential risk.

TALKING OUT OF TURN: PRIOR RESTRAINTS

If the First Amendment protects nothing else, it protects the right to speak first and pay the consequences later. Only in the rarest circumstances may government power be used to directly block speakers from speaking. This is not to say that government, especially the judicial branch, is not fond of trying. Lawyers themselves have been among the most frequent targets of judicially imposed "prior restraints." The flamboyant defense counsel to mobster John Gotti, for example, was convicted of contempt for violating a judge's order that he not be so brazen as to suggest publicly that his client did not commit a murder.

The criminal justice process is the most common setting for attempts at blocking the further dissemination of information. Courts have broad powers to order lawyers and law enforcement personnel to refrain from discussing cases outside the courtroom. This power may extend to witnesses and others, as well as to documents. However, once reporters or other members of the public have obtained information lawfully, judicial power to restrict its use is all but extinguished.

Journalists have successfully challenged judicial orders that go too far in restricting lawyers and others from talking to them about cases in progress, but such challenges are expensive and may prove unproductive. If someone who isn't supposed to talk does so anyway, there is no legal reason, apart from causing judicial irritation, that others, journalists included, cannot listen and use what they learn. Beware, however, of the potential for being subpoenaed when the court attempts to discover who committed the leak in violation of his order.

If a judge does order journalists or other members of the public to keep quiet about what they already have seen or heard, even though the order is almost certainly invalid, penalties for contempt may be enforced if the order is violated without any attempt having been made to get it set aside. How far to go in challenging an invalid order and how long to wait for a response are difficult questions. At a minimum, whatever options for appeal or other review of an order are available before the information would otherwise be disseminated should be pursued.

The other cases in which attempts to gag the press most frequently have been made involve purported threats to national security. It is true, perhaps, that loose lips can sink ships, and few would contend that the First Amendment immunizes the publication of information about troop movements or other military operations that would directly jeopardize lives. However, the threat of prior restraints seems to arise most often for the purpose of protecting political, not military maneuvers. The attempt to block the publication of the vast research report on the Vietnam War known as the Pentagon Papers is the best known, and was rejected by a divided Supreme Court. Other attempts at prior restraints have been justified as necessary to protect privacy; so far, these attempts have met with little success, but a few have been vigorously litigated at great expense to the media.

Occasionally, a court will attempt to condition a reporter's right to obtain information on an agreement not to use it. For example, courts sometimes have required persons who want to attend a proceeding involving a juvenile to agree in advance not to use the juvenile's name. In all cases, there are less draconian means of controlling access to those few facts that are truly sensitive, and journalists should agree to remain silent only after the most careful consideration. To the extent that such schemes purport to bar the use of information already lawfully obtained, they appear clearly unenforceable.

There is a final form of prior restraint that should not go unmentioned: killing the messenger. Each year at the annual meeting of its members, the Associated Press reports on those of its correspondents who died in the line of duty during the preceding year. At the 1994 meeting, the number was five. Speaking freely has a price, and sometimes it is a very high one.

V

ACCESS TO INFORMATION

THE FIRST AMENDMENT is not a freedom of information act. The Constitution may limit government's power to block citizens from speaking, but it leaves wide latitude to bar access to the raw materials that inform speech. Still, the ability to use federal and state public records and open meetings laws and a host of other statutes and regulations that affect public and private attempts at secrecy is a great asset to practitioners of free speech. Indeed, the Constitution itself may be read to favor, and sometimes even to mandate, access to information, especially judicial proceedings and records.

Before stepping into the quicksand of access law, every citizen seeking to be informed about public issues should note this caveat:

> The law is no substitute for intelligent persistence in uncovering information.

Indeed, any attempt to utilize the law's resources will be successful only as it complements the application of intelligent persistence. Any seeker of information should begin with careful consideration of what information is needed, where it resides, and who might be cajoled or coerced into providing it. None of the legal rules requiring open government compels the government to formulate questions for you or to keep its records in a manner that makes it easy to discern the answers.

A reporter or activist who demands of a city manager, "Why did you build that street there? Didn't you know about the spotted owl nests?" should not be surprised to receive in response a curt, "No comment!" A quiet request of a clerk for a copy of the environmental-impact statement on the Audubon Street extension

61

project will be more productive, and, if it isn't, a finger pointed to a passage or two in the state's public-records act will.

To lay the groundwork for getting information, pay attention to these principles:

- If a request is denied, do not take a lower-level bureaucrat's no for an answer. Pursue it up the chain of command. If the answer is still no, make dark noises about what a smart lawyer you have and urge reconsideration.

- Always assume that everything is public. If the keeper of the information disagrees, it is her chore to prove that you cannot have it.

- Press for the reason for any denial. When you know why a request is being denied, you, or your lawyer, will have an easier time refuting the denial.

- Formulate your requests for information carefully and precisely. No law says bureaucrats cannot be cute in turning down requests or pretending that information does not exist. Imprecise requests invite nonresponsive answers.

- As soon as you sense the likelihood of opposition, put the request in writing. The wording of a written request carries no special magic, but the more informed your request sounds, the more seriously it will be considered. The Reporters Committee and other resources listed in Appendix B offer form letters that easily can be adapted to your purpose.

- Assume that being polite and understanding will work better than coming on like Sam Donaldson with a migraine. Most government employees, and their lawyers, understand their legal duties and try to comply with them. If they like you well enough, they might help even if the law says they do not have to or should not.

When all else fails, do not be afraid to come on like Sam Donaldson with a migraine. The First Amendment may not be a freedom of information act, but the Constitution is a bar to jailing citizens for obnoxious curiosity.

COURT PROCEEDINGS
AND RECORDS

Statutes requiring public access usually do not apply to the judiciary. The Constitution does, however, and has been held to require public proceedings. Common law principles also mandate public access to courts. In most cases, unfortunately, such rights of access have been held to be conditional: a judge can get around them if he determines that the interest in secrecy is sufficiently compelling to outweigh the interest in public access.

The standard used in this balancing act may appear somewhat opaque. The Supreme Court has held that a "presumption of openness" applies to criminal proceedings, which "may be overcome only by an overriding interest based on findings that closure is essential to preserve higher values and is narrowly tailored to serve that interest." In fact, "overriding interests" are very rare. Closure seldom has been found "essential to preserve higher values" or "narrowly tailored" enough to pass muster. If this standard, or one similar to it, is applicable, closure is nearly impossible to sustain.

There is no doubt that the standard applies to all criminal trials, and to certain pretrial and posttrial proceedings, including jury selection. Though the Supreme Court hasn't ruled on the issue, few doubt that it applies to civil trials, as well.

The number of peripheral court proceedings that are not themselves "trials," however, is large, and the standards that should govern access to such proceedings frequently are disputed. The presumption always should be that the proceeding should be open, if the judge is present, unless there is a compelling reason for secrecy. Journalists and others who want to attend have the right to present arguments in favor of openness and to have the reason for closure set forth on the record.

Judges are fond of doing business in their "chambers," as judges' private offices are known, often with counsel, the parties, and a court reporter present. They also like to call counsel to the bench, or "sidebar," to consult, sometimes in whispered tones, so that jurors or others in the courtroom cannot hear what is said. Much of what happens in chambers or at the sidebar may rival in insignificance what goes on at the mound when a manager is making a pitching change. Also, many judges who use such settings for convenience will open the proceedings, if it is apparent that anyone cares to hear them. Simply moving the proceedings to chambers or the sidebar does nothing to change the standards of openness that should apply, but journalists should weigh carefully whether to challenge incidental private conversations unless there appears to be a pattern of abuse.

Courtrooms are imposing places, and some judges revel in the ceremony of robes and exclamations from the bailiff of "All rise!" They especially may like to be addressed as "Your Honor," and some will instruct the bailiff to make sure no one is reading newspapers, conferring with seatmates, or consuming donuts and coffee while the court is in session. None of this, however, should prevent a reporter or other citizen from objecting when the court clears the courtroom or announces that when court reconvenes it will do so in secret. Some news organizations provide little wallet cards to their reporters from which they can read a boilerplate objection to closure.

No magic words are necessary. The basic colloquy goes something like this:

"Your Honor, may I be heard?"

[Hearing someone speaking from behind the bar, the judge, and everybody else in the courtroom, is likely to turn toward the voice, with a look of either wonderment or pain. Several responses from the judge are possible, including, "No" or "Bailiff, arrest that wretch." Let's save the discussion of what to do in the event of a hostile response for a moment and presume the judge does the proper thing.]

"State your name for the record, please."

"Judie Citizen. That's C-I-T-I-Z-E-N, Your Honor."

"Yes. What is it?"

"I wish to be present during this proceeding and I would like an opportunity to be heard on why I believe the proceeding should be open to the public."

"Make it quick."

"If you could postpone the proceedings for an hour or two, I could have my lawyer present." [The judge may well grant this request, but let's presume she does not.]

"I'm sorry, but that's not possible."

"Well, then, let me just say that I believe these proceedings are subject to a presumption of openness, that can be overcome only by a showing—on the record, Your Honor—of a compelling need for closure. I do not believe that showing has been made."

"Is that all?"

"Yes, Your Honor. Thank you."

If you cannot find a way to state your objection orally, either because the cat got your tongue or the courtroom door already was locked, scribble it down on a piece of paper and ask the bailiff to give it to the judge. Do not be surprised if your argument fails to win a quick reversal of a judge's determination to proceed in secret. You have done all you can to lay the basis for a formal legal challenge to her decision.

Judicial records, as well as proceedings, are subject to a presumption of openness, but the presumption may have less weight, since the Supreme Court has ruled it comes only from common law and not the Constitution. The Court said the common law right of access is "not absolute" and that "the decision as to access is one best left to the sound discretion of the trial court, a discretion to be exercised in light of the relevant facts and circumstances of the particular case." Some lower courts have been generous in expanding the contours of the common law right of access and most have been loath to deny access to any records that actually are entered into the record of a trial.

What the law allows you to see, it does not necessarily permit you to copy. Most clerks' offices will make copies of their records for a fee; some have coin-fed copy machines available for the public. Some courts will provide copies by mail, if you know what you want and do not mind paying for it.

The proceedings themselves may be recorded in most states and photographed, but often under restrictive and arbitrary rules. The federal courts for the most part remain off limits to cameras and tape recorders. The Radio-Television News Directors Association (see Appendix B) has been a leader in bringing the judiciary into the electronic age and, along with state broadcast news organizations, can provide useful resources for obtaining electronic and film access.

GOVERNMENT MEETINGS
AND RECORDS

The records and meetings of most public agencies are governed by statutes that set the terms of access. These statutes share many common features, not the least of which is that they are all infernally complex and dreadfully boring. The best known and the most thoroughly explored by litigation is the Freedom of Information Act, passed by Congress in 1966. FOIA governs access to most federal government records. Meetings of federal agencies are governed by the Government in the Sunshine Act. Like state open-meetings laws, the Sunshine Act is often viewed by bureaucrats as a guide to how to operate in secret.

FOIA and the Sunshine Act do not apply to Congress, which knows better than to burden itself with the laws it imposes on others (state legislators typically do themselves the same favor in state open records and meetings acts). Since members of Congress, almost by definition, are incapable of keeping secrets, the omission is of little consequence. In addition to maintaining a steady flow of informal leaks, congressional staffs amass vast heaps of information to be printed by the Government Printing Office. If you cannot find a friendly congressional staffer who will give you such things for free, the GPO will sell it to you at a reasonable price per pound.

FOIA, like most state open-access laws, begins with the general proposition that everything is open. Then it proceeds to list the exceptions. California's Public Records Act, which was patterned on FOIA, has been estimated to be subject to over a thousand exemptions scattered throughout California law.

Even if the records you want are not exempt from disclosure, finding the agency, and the person within the agency, that has them may prove a challenge. FOIA requires most federal government agencies to publish their information-disclosure procedures in the *Code of Federal Regulations* (or *CFR*). *CFR* is many paperback volumes of agency rules on everything from hog price supports to fair housing and is kept in most libraries. Changes to *CFR* rules are published in the *Federal Register,* a daily newsprint compendium that outdoes even the *Congressional Record* for sheer ponderousness, both in prose style and heft.

Quite often, the most direct route to information is picking up the phone and asking the person who answers, knowing that with luck and no more than four or five transfers, you might find what you seek. Showing up on the doorstep of the agency may work even better. Otherwise, some time spent with the *CFR* may provide the combination. One of the provisions of all agencies' disclosure rules, happily, is that if you ask the agency, it must give you a copy.

FOIA and most state public-records laws permit charging fees for searching, reviewing, and copying records. These fees can be substantial, especially if there are hourly charges for time spent searching for the records and then reviewing them in a further search for excuses not to deliver them. FOIA permits fee waivers for most noncommercial users. Each agency's fee structure is published in *CFR.*

There is another side to the right to charge fees. Under FOIA and many state access laws, a citizen who sues for access may recover legal fees. As a result, even the most impecunious information seeker may be able to persuade a lawyer to help.

The Reporters Committee for Freedom of the Press (see Appendix B) has produced excellent practical guides for exploiting FOIA and state access laws. Similar work has been done by state press and broadcast organizations that have analyzed the details of their states' records and meetings laws (some examples are cited in Appendix B).

FOIA and other laws favoring public access were intended to counter the instinctive desire of all governments to conduct their business protected from the sanitizing glare of public scrutiny. In addition to maintaining information about its own business, government also serves as a repository of information about the businesses of others, records of real property, for example, and marriage, birth, and death records. Until recently, there was little question that such records were available to everyone. After all, if the government knows you were born a bastard, married by a justice of the peace, and had a driver's license restriction for eyeglasses, what more harm could result if your neighbor stopped by the courthouse and learned these truths?

As such records have multiplied and the power of computers to retrieve and match them has grown, an increasing popular revulsion has swept up to repress their use. Thus, it seems, for every new law requiring public access, there are ten designed to protect the privacy of information in government files (as though anything in the files of the government—who else is legally empowered to use armor, artillery, and gas chambers to enforce its will?—could be truly private). Motor vehicle records, voter registrations, postal forwarding information, even the identity of jurors have all been subject recently to legislative or judicial attempts to suppress truthful data.

Writers and speakers should be careful not to inflame public fears by carelessly misusing such data. At the same time, no one should be allowed the nostalgic notion that individuals have a right to remain ciphers to their fellow citizens. Not, at least, in a society with its roots in small towns where everyone knew who wore bifocals and how many cans of what kind of beer they consumed each week.

PUBLIC PLACES

Owners may control access to property. Private property owners usually have broad rights to exercise this control arbitrarily and capriciously and to enforce their rights through the law of trespass (see the discussion in the chapter on "News-Gathering Fouls"). Public property "owners" (those public officials who maintain custody of property in the public's behalf) also may limit access in a manner consistent with the nature of the property, subject to limitations imposed by the duties to permit free expression and avoid discrimination.

Reporters and other citizens are free to observe or record that which would be visible or audible from public thoroughfares. They may not be blacklisted from visiting government facilities or government-sponsored events, such as press conferences, on the basis of what they have published or might be expected to publish in the future. Access to crime and disaster scenes under the control of public authorities frequently is accorded to members of the press pursuant to state laws or local policies, though the police have broad powers to restrict such access. Schools and other government facilities normally not open to the public also may be subject to state or local laws or policies providing access for seekers of information, but there is little recognition of a broad constitutionally guaranteed right of access.

Jails and prisons present special problems, in part because of the perception of correctional authorities that attention from the press makes prisoners more difficult to control. The First Amendment has been asserted with little success as a basis for granting rights of access to correctional facilities and even to record the execution of the death penalty. Access to prisoners through the mail or by phone also is subject to broad restrictions that go with the loss of civil rights attendant to incarceration.

The best practical approach to gaining access to any site is simply to walk in, unless the presence of such deterrents as machine guns or Dobermans suggests the wisdom of being less direct. Do not ask permission if there is no obvious need to do so and do not

be devious, since burnt cork under your eyes and a camouflage
jacket tend to undercut the reasonableness of the presumption that
you had a right to be present. Be polite and confident in responding to any challenge and put the burden to the challenger of explaining why you shouldn't be there. Comply with a request to
move on if delivered by someone with clear authority or a questionable grip on his hair trigger.

Sites to which drawbridges already have been lifted present
greater challenges. A careful review of statutes, policies, and practices may reveal the basis for specific rights of access, or, at least,
for a contention that access is being denied on a discriminatory
basis. Finally, nothing pays like persistence and nothing shows persistence like the willingness to make a public stink about public
officials who try to conduct the public's business in secret.

PRIVATE-SECTOR INFORMATION

General Motors is not subject to the Freedom of Information
Act, nor is the weekly newspaper or the small private college in
Grinnell, Iowa, subject to the Iowa public-records law. Information
about all three may be maintained by public agencies, and some of
that information may be public because of FOIA or public-records
act rules applicable to those agencies. Other laws, especially the securities laws applicable to companies whose stock is held by the
public, may require GM to make information public. Laws requiring nonprofit institutions to reveal certain information may apply
to Grinnell College. Even the *Grinnell Herald-Register* may be required by postal laws, corporation codes, or local municipal li-
censing ordinances to open aspects of its otherwise private business to public scrutiny. If a private enterprise is involved in
litigation, it may be required to produce financial and other normally private data that could find its way into open public court
files or into the hands of lawyers who may share it freely with
friendly reporters.

Public activists and journalists should not expect to march into
private businesses and have the books turned open on the basis of

the First Amendment or state or federal laws aimed only at guaranteeing the accountability of public officials and government agencies. At the same time, everyone should be aware that little in this electronic, computerized world is truly secret in the face of spirited inquiry.

VI

THE RIGHT TO STAY SILENT

EVERYONE likes to complain about the growth in the number of lawyers. As with all parasites, however, the number of lawyers is directly proportional to the number of hosts: the real problem, if problem it be, is the proliferation of clients. Everybody wants to have a lawsuit, and a great many are fulfilling their wants.

One by-product of all this fulfillment is the high demand for witnesses. No lawsuit is worth its weight in briefs if it does not inconvenience dozens of otherwise innocent civilians who are cajoled or subpoenaed to receive their fifteen minutes of fame in the witness box. To satisfy this appetite, news organizations routinely provide volumes of business records, just as do other businesses, with a minimum of objection, apart from the occasional groans of overworked clerks slaving over copy machines. Journalists, however, greet the arrival of subpoenas with sharper noises, akin to the squeals of a stuck pig.

Journalists and others unfortunate enough to have reduced their thoughts and observations to paper or digital form are looked upon by lawyers as ideal witnesses: who better to explain how the accident happened than the reporter who wrote six paragraphs about it three years ago? Surely he remembers where every drop of blood was spilled and will testify as convincingly as any well-coached police officer as to how long the skid marks were.

The fact is that most reporters are lousy witnesses. The average reporter has written hundreds of six-paragraph reports over the last three years and has about as much memory of any one of them as Joe Montana has of a third-quarter incompletion in a meaningless game against the Colts in 1989. Worse, reporters, unlike quarterbacks, often feel professionally bound to pretend that they have good memories; unlike cops, they cannot easily be coached; unlike mobsters, they are easy to subpoena; and, unlike a high proportion of average citizens, they find it demeaning to lie under oath.

A subpoena is an order from a judicial or legislative body commanding a person to appear, either to give testimony or, if it is a subpoena duces tecum, to bring documents. A subpoena, while it summons, is not the same thing as a summons, which is a court order requiring a defendant to answer a lawsuit. Such terms may be used in different ways in different jurisdictions; one more reason to be careful in relying too heavily on a general work like this one. The rules under which subpoenas are issued, served, and enforced also vary somewhat from state to state or from court to court.

Reporters do have a degree of legal protection against being called to testify about their work; some of that protection may be claimed by others—scholars, for example—whose expressive work has led to a subpoena. In addition, there are practical tools that can reduce any unwilling witness's exposure to what the courts call "compulsory process."

PRACTICAL RESPONSES TO SUBPOENAS

The most obvious protection is this: *Do not talk.* Especially to lawyers or investigators who call to praise the excellent job you did on that little six-paragraph accident report or the incisive insights in your graduate thesis. When it is clear that a potential witness is going to be uncooperative, lawyers will cast about for easier, less expensive routes to present their cases.

In most cases, the legal barriers to reporter testimony do not occur to lawyers who happen on a crisp black-and-white article or a colorful piece of videotape that appears to describe a key feature of the case in authoritative terms. At most, they have some vague notion that journalists won't reveal their sources, but they're not interested, they say, in secret sources or confidential information; they just want testimony as to what was observed at the scene or stated on the record by participants, most of which is already in the published report. If an effusively flattering approach to the reporter elicits a warm feeling of inordinate self-importance, many of the practical and legal barriers to appearing in court may dissolve. So, for criminy's sake, keep your mouth shut. If you must say something, suggest the caller talk to your lawyer or your superior. In a majority of cases, the prospect of being compelled to testify will disappear right there.

Compelling a reluctant witness to testify requires careful negotiation of a tricky legal maze. Most lawyers will have trouble getting all the way through it and potential witnesses have no obligation to be helpful. For example, in many states, subpoenas must be served personally, physically handed to the recipient. Process servers, the people who get paid by lawyers to chase down witnesses and lay paper in their hands, are not high on the legal food chain. Some are very professional and very effective, but most aren't. When one arrives at the reception desk and asks to see reporter Jones, reporter Jones has no obligation to invite him up for coffee or come down to shake his hand. When the process server seeks out reporter Jones at home, and reporter Jones's significant other goes to the door, the process server may be told politely or otherwise to take a hike.

The persistent process server will not be deterred and sooner or later will nail reporter Jones. Not all process servers are persistent, and, if nothing else, the lawyer seeking the testimony will get the message that reporter Jones will be no more cooperative on the witness stand than she is while being chased through the bushes by the process server.

Do keep in mind that process servers, unlike most reporters, are sometimes unafraid to lie under oath and may testify that papers were served properly when they only were left on the receptionist's desk. Moreover, the process server may catch you on the porch picking up your morning newspaper on the same day the subpoena says you're supposed to be in court, thus making it difficult to find competent counsel who can explain effectively the various legal theories which limit a reporter's duty to testify. Another reason why it is a good idea to alert your own lawyer, if you're well-heeled enough to have one, as soon as you think that someone is seeking your testimony.

Your lawyer will want to know several things:

- What did the published report, if there was one, say?

- What is the nature of the case, what court is hearing it, and for what purpose is the testimony being sought?

- What other knowledge besides that published in your report do you have?

- What notes, drafts, outtakes, or other materials do you have that could have a bearing on the case?

- What have you said to the lawyers or parties involved in the case?

- What understandings do you have with persons connected with the case about what you can reveal—in other words, are there secret informants or confidential information that you have promised not to disclose?

- What reservations or policies do you or your employer have about how far you are willing to go in disclosing unpublished information, whether or not that information is confidential?

Your lawyer may not understand that he wants to know all this, so tell him, even if he does not ask.

Some of these answers bear on the legal arguments the lawyer might make; others will inform the practical strategies the lawyer might employ. For example, a subpoena to a reporter from the government in federal criminal proceedings must be approved personally by the attorney general (the rules are set forth in the *Code of Federal Regulations*), a fact that government lawyers may conveniently forget.

The most important practical strategy, however, depends upon none of the above. It is simply this: *Drag your feet.* The longer your appearance in court can be delayed, the more likely the lawsuit will be resolved or that the need for your testimony will abate. Seldom, however, should your dragging feet be set in concrete (as they will be, if you work in a newsroom that has an unfortunate penchant for written policies that read like something Moses found on the mountain). Journalists and others prone to indulge in expressive behavior, as well as aggressive litigators, relish the image of themselves being carried off on their bloody shields. In the matter of avoiding testifying, as well as so many other things in life, it is better to avoid provoking needless confrontations, especially with judges, who hold the power to send you directly to jail without even the opportunity to grab your toothbrush, let alone pass Go.

Equipped with your answers to her questions, your lawyer should have several cards to play before wasting time with legal research. Often, the lawyer seeking the testimony, call him Lawyer Larry, will be mollified by a simple affidavit, or declaration, attesting that:

- As a reporter, you never testify about confidential or unpublished sources or information.
- You wrote the attached report.
- It is your practice to report what you know accurately.
- You followed your practice when you wrote this report.

If Lawyer Larry will accept such an affidavit, it may be in your interest to give it to him. You do not even need a lawyer of your own to negotiate such a solution, though it is always better to have one, or to have an editor handle the negotiations for you.

Lawyer Larry may be more willing to accept such an affidavit if he knows one or more of the following facts, which he may learn from a carefully considered conversation with your lawyer:

- You would love to testify about all the scumbucket things you know about Lawyer Larry's client and you're dying to get on the stand to spill your guts.
- You cannot remember anything about the report—your only clue that you wrote it is your byline—and, if you were on the stand, your nervous titter and your complete lack of recollection are bound to convince the jury that the report itself is incredible.
- You, and/or your employer, are prepared to spare no legal expense in opposing your testimony and it will be a cold

and expensive day in hell before Lawyer Larry will get so
much as the proper spelling of your name out of you.
• You have no notes or other materials that could shed any
further light on what already is published in the report.

Your lawyer also may try being helpful by explaining to Lawyer
Larry various approaches to convincing the judge that the report
alone may be admitted as evidence without the need for testimony
from a reporter. Never underestimate the possibility that lawyers
making strident demands simply lack the competence to achieve
their goals peacefully. In fact, no lawyer may have seen the subpoena or thought about its implications before it was served. Prosecutors and insurance defense counsel particularly are prone to
issue standing orders to paralegals and investigators to subpoena
everybody whose name is mentioned anywhere in the case files.

Photographs, notes, and other documents especially are prized
by the likes of Lawyer Larry, since they may carry a patina of credibility that the average scruffy ink-stained wretch lacks. Thus, these
precautions:

• Be consistent in eliminating from your files materials that
won't be useful in the future.
• Consider returning documents no longer needed to the
source.
• Do not accept originals of documents or copies that easily
can be traced to a source to whom confidentiality is
important.
• Consider a practice of providing to the public, for sale or
otherwise, copies of only those photographs that have
been published (in the alternative, be prepared to provide
in response to a subpoena any photograph that otherwise
would have been offered for sale).
• Be careful what you put in your notes, especially, if you
intend to keep them around for more than a day or two.
• Never assume that any piece of paper, no matter how
humble (restaurant and gasoline receipts, little yellow
sticky things, the second calendar you keep at home, your
diary), won't be ferreted out and ordered into court.

Remember, if something disappears once you know a lawyer is looking for it, judges get especially irate, whether or not you have stepped so far over the line as actually to have committed the felony of destroying evidence.

At last we come, almost, to the law. First, though, a final tactical question: when to ask the judge to rule on whether the law permits a journalist to be forced to answer? The attraction of the bloody shield image would counsel this answer: at the earliest possible juncture. Most always, however, it is better to wait until the questions are asked before seeking a ruling on their propriety. Delay is consistent with the overall strategy of foot-dragging. Second, it forces Lawyer Larry to take his own chances about what might happen in a courtroom, perhaps with a jury present, chances that he may choose ultimately not to take. Third, and most important, as a matter of general principle, judges cannot understand why reporters should have any special privileges. However, in the context of an unfolding trial, the use of reporters as witnesses often seems unnecessary, a form of grandstanding or a needless distraction, and the judge will bend over backward to find a way to eliminate the distraction, even if the law isn't all that helpful to the reporter.

LEGAL BARRIERS TO COMPELLING TESTIMONY

The law, in fact, can be very helpful. Few reporters ever are ordered to testify against their wills and fewer still are penalized for refusing to do so. The problem is that the law is not simple and clear-cut and this can be frustrating to reporters just as it is to other citizens with a low tolerance for ambiguity. Most of the time the outcome hinges on a judicial balancing of the need for the testimony against the intrusion on the reporter's ability to gather news. The outcomes of such balancing acts are difficult to predict in advance and depend too much on subjective factors to give reporters much comfort, even those whose toothbrush is already packed.

The law affecting a subpoenaed reporter can be found in several places. The First Amendment places limits on reporter subpoenas, but courts vary widely in defining those limits and the consensus of most media lawyers is that it would not be wise to ask the Supreme Court to clarify the matter. The rules of evidence, which govern a court's decisions about the admissibility of all testimony, provide a fertile ground for barriers to access to reporter's files and memories; these rules are complex and technical and subject to endless local variations. Quashing a subpoena on a technicality may lack high drama, but it gets the job done.

Many state constitutions and statutes place explicit limitations, some of which are quite broad, on reporter subpoenas, and news organizations have had success convincing legislatures to refine and broaden those limitations. Sporadic efforts to persuade Congress to enact a federal "shield law" limiting reporters' obligation to testify in federal courts have not been successful, in part because some news organizations have expressed a questionable preference for relying on the First Amendment.

All of these limitations are strongest in cases where reporters are trying to protect highly sensitive information, particularly confidential sources, or where the need for the information is hard to establish. Some shield laws apply by their terms only to confidential sources, while others, like California's, are virtually absolute, unless the journalist is a party to the lawsuit or a criminal defendant is exercising the Sixth Amendment right to call the reporter as a witness in his defense. The other cases in which reporters have had the most difficulty avoiding the sound of clanging bars are those in which the judicial or legislative body is seeking testimony about violations of its own rules, especially secrecy rules. The celebrated case of California reporter Bill Farr, who spent forty-five days in jail, concerned his unwillingness to tell who had broken the judge's own rule forbidding release of information about a case.

In its most general terms, the legal argument in opposition to an attempt to compel testimony goes like this:

The law respects the needs of lawyers, ministers, spouses, and others whose special relationships cannot be preserved without the ability to protect confidences. The First Amendment extends a similar limited privilege to news reporters to refuse to divulge information that might damage their ability to gather news. At a minimum, this privilege requires the court to examine with care a claim of journalistic privilege and to take into account these factors:

- The importance of the information sought; does the information go to the heart of important issues or is it only of peripheral significance?

- The availability of other sources for the information; have those been exhausted?

In states with shield laws or court decisions recognizing special protection for news gatherers, the argument is similar but more compelling.

The best defense against reporter subpoenas is the one reporters like least to think about: the sure knowledge among judges that reporters will go to jail before they will reveal confidential information or sources. Journalists themselves differ widely in their interpretations of the duty to respond to subpoenas, but they are mostly unanimous on the ultimate issue: They will not break a promise of confidence, even if it means spending time in jail.

Do not forget that a finding of contempt and the jail term or fines that go with it aren't the only clubs available to loosen a reluctant witness's lips. When, as in a libel suit, the reporter or his news organization is the defendant, a judge may go so far as to enter judgment in favor of the plaintiff if a reporter refuses to give up information. The penalty for silence in such a case is not jail time but a crushing damages award that can destroy the news organization.

RULES FOR TESTIFYING

An order to testify may not be the end of the world. Thousands of reporters have testified without betraying confidences or damaging their ability to gather news in the future. Certain basic rules of testimony should be kept in mind by all witnesses, especially reporters. The first is to be represented, if at all possible, by competent counsel who understands and respects the ethical and legal rules surrounding reporter testimony. Most lawyers, even those who should know better, have difficulty fully assimilating these rules; a few err in the other direction and make First Amendment mountains out of cases that could have been resolved with a simple affidavit. Like other service providers (your mechanic, for example), your lawyer may need careful monitoring. In the end, though, listen closely to the advice and do your best to comply; the alternative is like fixing your own brakes.

Other useful rules of testimony:

- Your job is to answer questions, not to please the questioner. Avoid the understandable psychic urge to be liked by the person examining you.

- Do not attempt to answer questions that are unclear. Make the examiner ask the question he wants answered; do not help by volunteering the answer to a question you think he wants answered.

- Do not guess. If the answer is, "I'm not sure," that is the answer. Do not speculate about what might have happened. Remember, you do not care if the examiner likes you or respects your memory.

- Unless your lawyer advises you differently, do not prepare for your testimony by lying awake at night racking your brain for memories or going through old documents looking for answers to questions that might be asked. You're not obligated to have a good memory and efforts at reconstructing events may lead only to a false sense of certainty.

- Do not try to outsmart the questioner or impress her with your wit. Lawyers, even dumb ones, are better at this stuff than you are (how else do they get away with charging their rates?) and your efforts at wit usually will backfire.

- Answer only the question asked. Do not volunteer. Do not worry about the need to fill dead air. Long silences show up on transcripts as nothing more than a carriage return.

- Tell the truth.

Except for the last one, rules like these are general principles, not absolutes. Keep in mind your goal, which is to be as effective as possible in gathering and disseminating news and information. Listen carefully to counsel and keep a cool head. If nothing else, the experience will leave you a little less smug the next time you are called upon to report the cross-examination of a key witness by a congressman or district attorney.

SEARCH WARRANTS

Subpoenas for testimony aren't the only devices available for squeezing information out of unwilling providers. Search warrants may be used where information in the hands of news organizations is thought by prosecutors to be relevant to a criminal proceeding. The tactic is likely to backfire (editorial cartoonists have a field day depicting deputies digging through newsroom wastebaskets), and is strictly limited by a federal law, the Privacy Protection Act of 1980, and a number of state statutes. The act isn't limited to journalists and newsrooms but applies to any search for materials intended for public communication.

Prosecutors and judges often have forgotten, honestly or conveniently, the Privacy Protection Act, and there are special circumstances under which a newsroom search can be conducted without offending the act. Thus, it is a good idea to remember a few principles in case officers show up on your doorstep waving search warrants:

- Ask for a copy of the warrant and time to examine it. Also ask for, but don't expect to receive, time to consult a lawyer.

- Ask for credentials from each member of the search team and record the officers' identities.

- Accompany the officers throughout the search, making careful notes and, if possible, recording (including video) everything that happens.

- Do not obstruct or assist the officers (if they insist on breaking open desks or doors, offer them the keys, but make sure it is clear that you are not consenting to anything they do).

- Do nothing that could be construed as destroying evidence (deleting computer files is just as destructive as feeding documents to a shredder).

If a search occurs, you can take solace in the knowledge that the Privacy Protection Act permits those who suffer trespasses in violation of the act to recover damages and attorney fees. The Minneapolis Star and Tribune Co. successfully extricated over $80,000 in fees and damages from the FBI following an ill-advised search.

VII

INFORMATION AS PROPERTY

SOME PRACTITIONERS of free speech are more interested in being heard than in getting paid for their efforts, but few will turn down offers of cash. The challenge in this age of photocopiers and fiber-optic highways is how to collect tolls from users who pass like cat burglars in the night. However inadequate it may be, the law of copyright usually holds the combination to the vault, though other legal theories also may establish a right to demand payment for images or text.

Few speakers and writers need be drawn into the deeper box canyons of intellectual property law, but a knowledge of some basic concepts is necessary to avoid embarrassment and impoverishment. Keep in mind that this chapter, more than most, skims the surface of a complex and fluid body of law plumbed to its depths only by specialists.

COPYRIGHT PROTECTION FOR CREATORS

The power to protect copyrights and patents is one of the specific grants of authority accorded to Congress by the Constitution:

> To promote the progress of science and useful arts, by securing for limited times to authors and inventors the exclusive right to their respective writings and discoveries.

In carrying out that authority, Congress enacted the first Copyright Act in 1791. The current version is the Copyright Act of 1976, enacted after decades of legislative gridlock to replace the act of 1909, under which works as diverse as Edith Wharton's *Age of Innocence* and the Rolling Stones' "Sticky Fingers" had been recorded for protection.

A "work" subject to copyright protection is defined in the act as an "original work of authorship fixed in any tangible medium of expression." Authorship is a broader concept than "writing," the term used in the Constitution and in earlier copyright acts, and encompasses such nonliterary works as computer programs. Diagrams, maps, photographs, sculpture, and other graphic or artistic works are subjects of copyright. So are audiovisual works, melodies, and lyrics. Names, titles, and short phrases are not copyrightable, but they may be subject to other legal protections. Most notably, ideas and facts are not copyrightable, only the tangible form in which they are expressed.

The work becomes subject to protection at the instant it is fixed in tangible form, as, for example, with each keystroke of a word processor. An author today need do nothing more than type or scrawl out words; copyright protection flows automatically from creation. Proof of the creator's rights may be easier to establish, however, if certain steps are followed.

The most basic is the intellectual equivalent of a cattle brand: the copyright notice displayed prominently on any copies of the work that may be seen by others. Notice requirements once were highly technical and the consequences of distribution without a notice, even if accidental, severe. On all works created after March 1, 1989, a notice is not a prerequisite to a creator's claim of rights, but its presence is a sure mark of the creator's intent. This is the typical form:

Copyright 2001 Arthur C. Author

The symbol © may be used in place of the word copyright. The additional expression "all rights reserved" may be added to perfect claims in some international jurisdictions. The notice should appear prominently at the beginning of the work.

The old trick of mailing a copy to yourself and keeping it in its sealed post-marked envelope is a cheap and easy way of establishing the date of authorship. Proof of priority may be invaluable in an infringement suit.

Actually registering a work with the Copyright Office is unnecessary to establish ownership, and few creators bother with it before commercial publication. Registration is, however, a prerequisite for commencing a lawsuit against an infringer. Also, once a work is registered, subsequent infringements give rise to damages set by the statute and attorneys' fees, regardless of whether the owner can prove actual harm.

The Copyright Office publishes its rules in the *Code of Federal Regulations,* and you can write or call for a copy of its registration procedures, forms, and a schedule of fees: Copyright Office, Library of Congress, Washington, DC 20559 (202-479-0700).

Under American law, those who create works during an employment relationship—most newspaper or television reporters, for example—have the least stake in that part of copyright law that defends the rights of creators: They do not own anything that can be stolen. If a work is "made for hire," the presumption of the Copyright Act is that ownership is in the hirer, not the hiree. Employees are hirees; their employers are presumed to retain all ownership rights in the works. The only significant exception applies when there is a written agreement reversing the presumption. If, on the other hand, a work is not "made for hire," the presumption is that the creator—a freelance, for example—retains all rights absent a written agreement to the contrary.

Employees and employers should take care to clearly delineate their respective ownership rights. An employee who writes a book on his own time, for example, may want to obtain a written acknowledgment from his employer that the book will not be deemed a work for hire, or keep careful records that show the work was performed on weekends or after hours.

"Copyright" is a collection of rights in a single work. Those rights can be sold one at a time. For example, "one-time newspaper publication rights" can be sold by a freelance to a newspaper. The freelance can resell the same rights to another newspaper, or, if he gets lucky, he can sell "North American motion picture rights" to Robert Altman and "exclusive book rights throughout the world" to Andrews and McMeel. Maybe he also can peddle the music rights and the stage performance rights and all manner of other rights to a long line of well-heeled benefactors.

Unless the copyright owner signs a written agreement specifically conveying broader rights, the presumption is that any sale of rights is for one-time use and is nonexclusive. Thus, if a newspaper buys a column for its editorial page, without a further written agreement, the newspaper may not have the authority to convey reprint rights to a third party, or even to give permission to a teacher who wants to distribute copies to a class. Those rights remain with the creator.

The precise wording of contract clauses conveying rights is critical to determine who owns what, especially with the rapid change in the technology of information distribution. Both sellers and buyers must ensure that any document transferring rights, even an informal submission letter or note of acceptance from an editor, carefully identifies the scope of the rights affected.

Assigning value to rights is difficult. Creators, of course, worry that they are selling too cheaply or giving away rights that someday will prove immensely valuable. The burgeoning of the information superhighway heightens these fears, as publishers try to market databases of information obtained in the past, and the posting of a photograph on an obscure computer bulletin board in Missoula makes it available to anyone in the world with a modem. It probably is self-serving for a publisher's lawyer to suggest that a bird in the hand is worth two in the bush, but creators who hold out too strongly for more favorable rights agreements may forgo cash sales today chasing a tiny stake in a hypothetical pot of gold. Publishers face the other side of the same dilemma, fostering paperwork nightmares and risking good relationships with creators to position themselves for participation in a marketplace with unproved rewards.

Copyrights do not last forever; figuring out how long is surprisingly complicated, depending on by whom and when the work was created. For works created by an identified individual on or after January 1, 1978, the term under the 1976 act is the life of the creator plus fifty years.

A work need not be published to be protected from infringers. Letters and diaries, for example, are subjects of copyright, and use without the permission of their owners may be infringing. In addition to damages for infringement, owners of unpublished works may seek injunctions to bar publication. The owner of copyright, in a letter, unless the rights have been transferred, is the writer, not the recipient. The recipient does own the paper and ink and can sell those to a third party, an autograph collector, for example, but she cannot convey the right to publish the letter's contents. Before the act of 1976, most unpublished material was not subject to infringement because it usually lacked the notices that then were a prerequisite to the assertion of rights. Few courts have considered the effect of this new rule on business correspondence and other documents that figure prominently in investigative reporting and civic watchdog activities.

RIGHTS OF BORROWERS

Successful creators borrow from each other. No work is ever entirely original. The Copyright Act extends protection only to the form in which intellectual property is fixed, not to ideas or facts. Anyone can write a play about an over-the-hill salesman, but calling him Willy Loman and lifting lines or specific situations from Arthur Miller's work may be held to infringe his rights in *Death of a Salesman.*

Borrowing ideas is not an infringement because ideas and facts are not subject to copyright. Specific lines or situations *are* subject to copyright, but the right to borrow them is acknowledged by the Copyright Act's provision for "fair use." Generally, lifting a small portion of a copyrighted work for use in a manner that does not impair the economic value of the original is a fair use. Unfortunately, "fair use" remains vague and difficult to apply in the real world.

Quoting from a book in a review or reprinting a few paragraphs from a textbook chapter for distribution to a high school class is fair use. Only a small proportion is taken and economic harm to the original is nonexistent. Quoting a stanza from a brief poem or a line or two of a lyric from a popular song is more problematic, since the amount taken represents such a large proportion of the whole. Likewise, reprinting an entire chapter from a larger work, instead of asking students to buy the work, or the library to stock more copies for reserve reading, has a measurable, if small, impact on sales, making it hard to argue that the use does not impair economic value. Remember, the test isn't just the economic gain experienced by the infringer—a high school teacher who distributes photocopies of magazine articles is not enriched by the act—but economic harm to the creator, who loses sales when her work is given away by others.

Parodies of copyrighted works generally will be deemed to be fair uses of the original, so long as the parody is unlikely to be taken seriously, and the purpose is not to sell products or services.

COMMERCIAL APPROPRIATION AND OTHER CLAIMS

The Copyright Act precludes states from enforcing copyright protection under their own laws, but state law concepts of invasion of privacy and unfair competition often are employed in disputes about creative works.

The variety of invasion of privacy known as "commercial appropriation," recognized in many states, forbids the use of a person's name or likeness for commercial purposes. Names of companies and products and other "trade names" also may be protected from misuse under both state and federal trademark laws. Some points to note:

- Use of names and likenesses in news reports is not "commercial," even though a price may be charged to readers or viewers. Generally, a use is commercial when the purpose is to draw attention to a product or service or to imply an endorsement.

- Dead celebrities sometimes rise up to bite living publishers; the rules and interpretations vary from state to state, but you should assume that anyone who was prominent during the twentieth century has an heir out there waiting to give you a bad time.

- To prevent popular trade names, like Xerox and Jacuzzi, from becoming generic, owners must show that they have worked hard to defend the name; thus, squads of young lawyers are deployed to complain to publishers who permit the trademark Tylenol to be printed with a lowercase "t" or refer to spas as "jacuzzis." To avoid such hate mail, and, what is more important, out of respect for the precision of language, do not call plastic "Plexiglas" unless you're sure.

- If it can be construed to have sucked the commercial value out of the original, even an otherwise noncommercial use may lead to a viable claim. The classic case of this type, perhaps the only one, involved the broadcast of preeminent human cannonball Hugo Zacchini's "entire act" ("Boom!" "Whiz!" "Plop!") by a Cleveland television station. The lesson: Use the "Boom" and the "Plop" but leave the "Whiz" on the cutting-room floor.

- Proprietors of public spectacles, especially professional sports entrepreneurs, increasingly try to tie contractual strings to writers and photographers covering their events. Such strings are best discouraged by a consistent refusal to accept them, even if the result is no film of the game. The commercial realities work in your favor: the Chicago Cubs need free publicity more than you need free access.

Infringement of copyright and other rights in informative works occurs relatively unchecked, thanks to the irresistible lure of the photocopying machine and other vehicles of mass replication. Almost everyone at some time or other has copied a work and distributed it in a fashion that exceeds the bounds of fair use. Companies copy whole editions of expensive newsletters and distribute them to employees. Politicians and restaurateurs copy favorable editorials or reviews and mail them to prospective voters or customers. Teachers assemble textbooks out of photocopies of other works. Families buy one expensive software program and distribute copies to sons and daughters in college.

The economic harm to the creator may be rationalized away:

"Because little Johnnie got a free copy of Tetris, he's more likely someday to pay for an upgrade of his own"; or "Because a consultant passed out copies of a chapter from a Tom Peters's tome on management, the recipients are more likely to buy his book." That such rationalizations have a kernel of truth may be one reason why infringements are not more aggressively attacked, but it makes them no more defensible. When attacks are made, the "everybody else is doing it" defense is hollow as an empty toner cartridge.

VIII

LAWYERS AND LITIGATION

SOME WRITERS AND SPEAKERS may be fortunate enough to have legal counsel, whether supplied by employers or paid for out of the proceeds of movie rights or an inheritance, in time to provide prophylactic assistance. Some may be so unfortunate as to be defendants, the prophylactic having failed or been disregarded during a flurry of expressive activity. A satisfying relationship with counsel is not the product of divine grace; it requires study on both sides.

THE GOOD CLIENT

The quality and cost of legal services depend as much on the savvy of the client as on the sagacity of the lawyer. Clients must understand that legal advice is fact specific. The slightest shift in the facts can change completely the legal outcome. A lawyer's research memorandum begins with a statement of facts, then goes on to a legal analysis of those facts. Judges write their opinions the same way. If the facts are wrong, the legal analysis is worse than useless. To get good legal advice, a client must accurately and cogently state the facts on which that advice is based. To avoid misunderstanding, state the facts in writing at the outset, and double-check them in evaluating the advice.

Remember this exception to the rule that the law is entitled to every person's evidence: If you communicate with counsel to obtain legal advice, the contents of that communication usually are immune from disclosure to an adversary. To qualify for that immunity, written materials should be addressed to counsel and marked as attorney-client communications. Copies should not be circulated to anyone outside the chain of communication with the lawyer.

Lawyer and client often disagree about the scope of relevant factual inquiry. When the lawyer seems to be fishing for information that has no apparent relevance, the client should point out her reservations, but be prepared to devote the time needed to give the lawyer everything he requests. Too often, news reporters or editors expect a comprehensive legal answer to an incomprehensible question. Put another way, lawyers are dumb, especially when it comes to the realities of their client's professional lives; it is up to the client to educate them. The more the need for this education is met at the beginning of the relationship, the higher the quality of legal advice and the lower the cost.

The client's initial intense interest in the outcome of a legal issue may cool significantly as soon as that day's deadline has passed and she has moved on to another assignment. Meanwhile, the lawyer is running up a substantial bill and investing emotional energy only to find himself mounting the barricades, waving the flag, and turning around to see his bored brigade clustered around a faraway water cooler. This is distressing to publishers who must pay the bills, but it is especially tiresome for house lawyers who do not get to send bills and must spend weekends completing newsprint purchase agreements put aside during their toil in the vineyard of press freedom. Good clients will not launch lawyers on crusades in which they themselves do not intend to participate.

THE COMPETENT COUNSEL

The law may be a seamless web, but no lawyer is equally familiar with all its strands. With each new legislative enactment or judicial decision, the web is extended and made more complex, and the task of the lawyer made more daunting. Even if all lawyers were equally well trained, equally smart, equally diligent, and equally ethical, no one of them would be equally suited to every task.

Almost all lawyers have law degrees and all have licenses from one or more states. A few are certified in such specialties as family law or have advanced legal degrees. Some went to law schools, like Harvard or Yale, that have almost impossibly demanding entry standards, and, therefore, produce graduates somewhat above the norm in sheer intellectual firepower. Some went to regional law schools, with modest entry standards and flexibility enough to accommodate part-time attendance. Many lawyers have attached themselves to huge law firms, whose names carry brand recognition, sometimes imply high standards of training and commitment, and always command a premium hourly rate. None of these background facts tells much about a particular lawyer's fitness for efficiently performing a particular task.

The best reference for any lawyer, just as for an ice-cream parlor, is a satisfied customer, particularly one who has faced the same problem that afflicts you. Next best, perhaps even better, is an unhappy competitor, one who has just been skunked by someone with a better tasting Rocky Road. If you have a First Amendment problem, call a local newspaper or broadcaster and ask for the names of their lawyers. Better still, find a trade association or a communications company and call their legal departments for references.

When you get a name or two, call them, briefly describe your problem, and ask them for references. You will find, if you poke around a little, that there are networks of lawyers who are experienced, or want to be experienced, in particular legal specialties. Once you tap such a vein, the supply of names will be endless. Many of them know each other and they tend to show up at the same bars, read the same publications, sport the same neckwear. Be careful, because all such networks are infused with competitive jealousies, old scores to settle, and a false sense of confidence in their own rumor mills. Everybody may think a certain New Yorker is the best First Amendment attorney on earth, and, while he may be very good, reputation becomes self-perpetuating: if he never takes another case and devotes himself to stamp collecting, his name still will be mentioned twenty years from now on the roster of great First Amendment attorneys and swarms will pound his door seeking advice.

The types of problems addressed in this book will excite the interest of most lawyers, who are sick of reviewing leases for strip malls and taking depositions of competing claimants for dear departed Aunt Elsie's certificates of deposit. They should be willing to listen as you briefly describe your problem. Avoid naming the guilty and describing the caliber of the murder weapon; keep the initial description to the broad outlines: "I publish a newsletter and I've been threatened with a suit for libel," or "I've written a novel and I have some concerns about copyright." Then put the shoe on the lawyer's foot. Explore the following:

EXPERIENCE. Though there are a few fine lawyers who make a living defending the First Amendment, most such cases are handled by attorneys whose primary experience is in other areas, especially general litigation. While lawyers must protect the confidences of their clients, they should be willing to list for you other cases they have handled and clients they have represented. Experience in even one or two matters similar to your own may be enough, if the lawyer is otherwise competent.

STAFFING. Unless you are talking to a sole practitioner, you have to watch for a bait and switch—great schmoozing from a weathered graybeard who signs you up, then passes you off to a greenhorn three months out of law school who will have a fine time learning all about the First Amendment at your expense. If you select a lawyer, you have the right to get the lawyer you selected, not her niece Hazel.

FEES. A lawyer-client relationship isn't much different from a contract for bathroom remodeling. Failure to reach a full understanding of the terms—"Oh, I had no idea you wanted a roof on it. That will be $2,000 more, please"—guarantees discord and dissatisfaction later. All aspects of the cost of legal services should be disclosed up front.

AVAILABILITY. Most good lawyers are overbooked. If they want your business, they will assure you they have time to handle it, whether they do or not. First Amendment legal problems look more interesting in the abstract than in the particular. The overbooked lawyer who could not resist the case when he first heard about it, may get lackadaisical when he is knee-deep in documents or depositions, or when he realizes that journalists and novelists are just as boring and not nearly as well-to-do as real estate developers and rich widows and widowers. The more promises of full commitment you can extract at the outset, the more embarrassed the lawyer will be to shortchange you down the road.

COMMUNICATION. You have a right, indeed a duty, to be fully informed about your lawyer's work on your behalf. Select a lawyer with whom you can communicate comfortably, one who will not talk down to you, but is willing to explain matters in understandable terms. One sign of such qualities is the presence of an earnest and capable secretary or personal assistant who will make sure that messages are accurately transmitted.

Fine lawyers can be found in both sole practices and huge law firms. What matters is not how many receptionists people the marbled reception area, or whether costs are held down by the use of a $39 answering machine in the kitchen. Favorable resolution of your problem will come from brainpower applied, your lawyer's and your own.

CONTROLLING COSTS

Law is like medicine. If the patient or client does not care about quality of life and is sufficiently motivated, and sufficiently rich, the number of nostrums and procedures applicable to a given problem is almost infinite. So is the cost. Since the cost of lawyers is directly proportional to the time they spend, the key to controlling costs is in making careful choices about how that time is invested.

Start with the realization that every legal problem, like every scrape and bruise, does not require professional intervention. A doctor's attention to a paper cut may save one case in of ten thousand of blood poisoning, but that one case does not justify the cost of ten thousand office visits. Give careful thought to the alternatives and the costs before calling a lawyer.

When the lawyer is called, be prepared to do everything you can to substitute your time for hers. An hour you spend collecting and organizing facts and narrowing the range of questions may save several hours the lawyer would otherwise spend trying to figure out what she was being asked. If you are drawn—kicking and screaming—into a prolonged legal relationship, say, to defend a libel suit, monitor the lawyer's work carefully to identify ways in which you can take over time-consuming tasks of gathering information, organizing files, making copies, or scheduling witness interviews.

Like doctors prescribing expensive tests, lawyers may want to plunge down many blind alleys, researching arcane points of law or going on fishing expeditions for remote facts. When one of these expeditions reveals the silver bullet that terminates the lawsuit, you may consider it money well spent, but many of these excursions are not cost-justified. The lawyer who fails to recommend them, like the doctor who fails to order an MRI, may worry about malpractice, or that he isn't on the cutting edge and risks derision from his peers. It is up to the client to be familiar with his own course of treatment and to work with the lawyer in choosing corners to cut.

Some things to look for:

UNNECESSARY LEGAL RESEARCH, especially when performed by junior associates. You have a right to know in advance what issues need to be researched, who will do it, and what it will cost. You also are entitled to see the product of these labors, usually in the form of legal memoranda. Asking for such things is the legal equivalent of making your mechanic show you the worn-out parts.

OVERAGGRESSIVE "DISCOVERY." Interviewing a witness informally is much less expensive than taking a deposition. Do not be afraid to exercise your own judgment about what information needs to be gathered and the most efficient way to gather it.

TOO MANY EXPERTS AND INVESTIGATORS. Ask for a clear explanation of why these are needed and what they will cost.

UNNECESSARY LEGAL MANEUVERS. Much of the high cost of legal services results from fierce infighting about peripheral issues. Whenever your lawyer wants to go see the judge about an issue, find out why and ask the lawyer to explain the alternatives.

MEANINGLESS PAPER. Insist on knowing in advance what legal documents are necessary, who is going to prepare them, and how much time they should take. You should see copies of all documents when they are completed, or, if you wish, in draft (since you probably are being charged for copies, you may want to review your lawyer's files in his office rather than demand copies to take home). You also should see copies of the opposition's documents.

Monitoring your lawyer's work not only lets you know what you are getting for your money, it also acts as a powerful incentive for the lawyer not to get sloppy. If no one questions the cost or need for a legal research project, or an extra couple of depositions, even the otherwise efficient and honest lawyer will err on the expensive side.

Many lawyers, especially those in large law firms, like to prattle on about saving the client money by assigning tasks to less-expensive junior lawyers. True, one hour of legal work at $100 is a better deal than the same hour for $300, but it isn't that simple. Some tasks will take the same amount of time no matter how experienced the lawyer, but most won't. In most cases, the client is better off to pay a higher rate to get a higher level of legal efficiency. Too often, the $100 lawyer spends $500 of your money spinning his wheels, before giving up in exasperation and spending $400 more ($100 on himself and $300 on the senior partner) having the senior partner spend an hour explaining how she could have done the whole job in thirty minutes. Good law firms write off some of this time, but the client is better served to insist at the outset that no work be done by anyone other than the principal lawyer without the client's approval.

Junior associates often are assigned to be present, sometimes in twos or threes, whenever the senior partner goes to court or to take a deposition. This may be to save workers' compensation claims from senior partners who hurt themselves carrying their own bags. Or it may be that senior partners need more moral support than the rest of us. But mostly it has to do with the same law firm economics that drives firms to be so helpful in shoving off tasks to less-expensive associates. The senior partners would rather make money off the associates than do the work themselves. Besides, a lawyer can only bill so much of his own time; he can add associates infinitely, and each one, especially after a year or two of seasoning, contributes about one-half of his billing rate to be divided among the partners. This isn't dishonorable; it is just the way the business works, and the client has only himself to blame if he does not guard against its consequences.

Finally, the hourly rate itself. Yes, it is negotiable, especially for clients who pay on time and have interesting work. First Amendment–related legal work is, on the whole, much more fun than writing wills. Not only does it amuse and stimulate the lawyers who do it, it also is a selling point for law firms trying to compete for the best associates. So, law firms, and lawyers, may be willing to take on a libel case for a lot less profit than they would demand of a slip-and-fall case. They won't think of it, though, unless you ask them, and show a willingness to take your business elsewhere if you do not get the answer you want.

While lawyers charge for most tasks by the hour, that isn't the end of it. Some have minimum charges, say a quarter hour, for any telephone call, no matter how brief. Most charge for such "extras" as photocopies and telephone charges, including faxes, often at ridiculous rates. All costs paid to third parties—for example, for court filing fees, court reporters, expert witnesses, investigators— are passed on directly to the client. If travel is involved, some will insist on first-class airfare and four-star lodgings and meals. The extras, like the hourly rate, are negotiable.

Most lawyers provide fully itemized bills showing the date, amount of time, and a description for all services charged, but a few still offer one-line bills—"Services rendered: $25,000"—unless the client demands more detail. Demand it.

INSURING THE RISK

Libel and other tort claims that arise out of the exercise of free speech are, like automobile negligence claims, insurable risks. Several insurance companies and a few specialized insurance brokers are in the business of selling coverage for libel and related torts. Most of their customers are commercial media organizations, but some can arrange coverage for individual authors or specific projects.

Most homeowners already have coverage for libel and are not even aware of it. The liability provisions of standard homeowner's insurance policies usually extend to claims for libel. Political candidates and others, such as letters-to-the-editor writers, who speak out for noncommercial reasons, may be able to call on their homeowner's insurance carrier for defense costs.

Insurance companies, of course, do not get rich holding out for principle or engaging the best—and most expensive—lawyers. That is why some news organizations have preferred to remain uninsured, or to use industry-captive insurance companies, so that the client retains control over the litigation—and settlement—of cases where high principle and professional reputation are paramount.

IX

KEEPING SPEECH FREE

IRONICALLY, journalists seem most inept when crusading for themselves. The language of the First Amendment aside, "No Law" is not the motto of Congress and the legislatures. Laws are passed all the time that diminish expression rights, and legislative initiatives that might benefit those rights often are met with no enthusiasm. The future of free speech depends on an active and informed constituency working to influence the legislative process to advance the cause. Without that effort, the list of legal obstacles will grow and legal protection of news gathering and dissemination will decline.

The First Amendment may be written on two-hundred-year-old parchment, but its nuances are not. Until World War I, only a handful of judicial decisions interpreted the First Amendment. Until 1931, the First Amendment was presumed to apply only to the federal government, not to state lawmakers. Until 1964, libel law was deemed to be exempt from the First Amendment. The Freedom of Information Act was not passed until 1966. The multitudes of other laws that influence public expression change almost daily, as legislators and judges tinker endlessly.

Much of the public policy debate about First Amendment issues turns, unfortunately, on the "rights" of the press, those arrogant banshees who are seen on television chasing fires, berating public officials, and hounding grieving funeral goers. Almost any issue that can be framed as a dispute between such hooligans and someone else is a winner for the someone else, even though the result may be a loss for all citizens who want to participate in public discussion.

There may have been a time when the press barons, like Hearst and Pulitzer and McCormick with their vaunted power to influence elections, threw a crumb or two to the First Amendment,

when they weren't tending to their real estate interests. Then came
television and the fragmentation of the electorate. Newspapers,
now, are just one of a number of ways to influence voters, and not
a very helpful one at that, since journalists' growing attachment to
objectivity and fairness make it damnably difficult to collect from
them for political favors.

When florists want to influence Congress, they send flowers
and dispatch as their emissaries small business men and women
from Racine or Topeka. Journalists, on the other hand, write ex-
posés about sexual peccadilloes or all-expense-paid junkets to the
Mediterranean and put Mike Wallace with a microphone in front
of the White House. Journalists, and many others who are vocal
about public issues, are not in the business of being nice. Florists
may not be nice, either, but they know that flowers curry more
favor than strident repetitions of the truth.

The point is not that journalists should ease up on investigative fervor. All lobbyists for First Amendment causes know one
thing for certain: The day they take hat in hand to beg help from a
congressman, the *Washington Post* that morning will carry at least
two investigative articles, an editorial, and a Doonesbury cartoon
questioning the congressman's virtue, to say nothing of his sanity,
patriotism, and relationships with barnyard animals. Nobody said
it would be easy to protect the First Amendment and improve the
climate for informed public discussion. Nevertheless, journalists
and others who care about free speech and recognize the power
that government officials have to undermine or exalt First Amendment values must also accept their own role as advocates for those
values.

Some things to keep in mind for those who seek to be effective
in advancing the cause of free speech:

HANG TOGETHER. Do not set yourself apart from other citizens.
Remember that "or of the press" is almost an afterthought in the
First Amendment guarantee of free speech for all citizens. Too
often, judges and other public officials see First Amendment claims
as special pleading by journalists or fanatics rather than a laudable
assertion of the rights of all.

PUT ON A HUMAN FACE. Gun manufacturers know they are not lovable. That's why the National Rifle Association works so hard to sign up individual citizens as members. When the NRA sends checks, the money may come mostly from manufacturers, but when it speaks, it speaks through the cards and letters and phone calls of millions of individual gun fanciers. Individual journalists and all speakers and writers should make their voices heard on First Amendment issues.

SING FROM THE SAME PAGE. The NRA may speak through individuals, but it does not leave what they say to chance. Professional organizations, like the National Association of Broadcasters, the Newspaper Association of America, state press and broadcast associations, the American Society of Newspaper Editors, and many others play a key role in framing debate. Speakers and writers who let the power in such organizations go by default to those who care only about convention junkets and economic issues have only themselves to blame for the lack of strong support for the First Amendment.

BUILD BRIDGES. When a good advocate speaks out for a cause, he does not just bash his opponents, he also reaches out for allies. Even the NRA and the tobacco lobby have an interest in free speech. The speech lobby, if there is one, should not fear calling for support on those whose primary aims may be distasteful. Politics makes strange bedfellows. Sharing the blankets need not lead to unsafe sex.

RUSH IS YOUR FRIEND. The First Amendment knows no left or right. Partisans are unanimous in their distaste for those who would let their enemies be heard. Do not let liberals, conservatives, atheists, Baptists, flat-earthers, or know-nothings forget that without a favorable environment for free speech they are all at greater risk.

SPEAK SOFTLY. Do not go out of your way to be obnoxious. The contrast between the unfailing politeness of Martin Luther King Jr. and the stridency of the Chicago Seven may explain why a national holiday celebrates King's birth and there is not an elementary school anywhere to be found with Abbie Hoffman's name above the door.

COMB YOUR HAIR. Appearances count, not just when you're standing before Congress, but when you are out in the street taking notes on a Fourth of July parade, filming children in line to see Santa Claus at the mall, or standing in front of the school board with an impertinent inquiry. Journalists and other writers and speakers are constantly on public view, either live or via videotape. Would your Aunt Alice approve of what she sees?

SWING YOUR BIGGEST STICK. If you buy ink by the barrel, splash it around. Cover your own disputes as news. Do it with the same objectivity you would cover any other political controversy, but do not shrink from putting First Amendment issues on page one and quoting yourself and your friends (on these issues, every right-thinking citizen should be your friend—some just won't know it until you tell them).

PONTIFICATE. If you editorialize and publish opinion pieces about foreign or monetary policy, do the same favor for the First Amendment, for improvements in libel law and access law. Punish unmercifully those who sin against the First Amendment, just as you would those who take the wrong side on a local zoning dispute. So what if most of your readers and viewers aren't interested; how many of them give a damn about the Federal Reserve?

CARDS AND LETTERS COUNT. Even if you only buy ink by the BIC, you can use it effectively in the cause of free speech. Write and call, not only politicians, but also editors and talk show hosts. With all the other nuts who sound off on the radio and in the letters-to-the-editor columns, why not those who care about greater access to government records and restrictions on libel damages?

TALK IT UP. Remember that for most people the First Amendment is an acquired taste. Time and resources devoted to education on the role of the First Amendment are well spent, even when not keyed to specific legislative or judicial disputes. Tell your Uncle Wayne about it at your next family reunion.

THEY WANT IT ON A PLATE. When McDonald's seeks a change in franchising law, it goes to legislators armed not only with lobbyists

and a lengthy record of campaign contributions, but with extensive evidence of the need for the change and articulate expositions
of how it can be accomplished without harm to any other public
interest. All the evidence and much of the exposition may be self-
serving and susceptible to logical attack, but that is beside the
point. You cannot get to first base with a legislator, especially one
you cannot pay, unless you do his work for him.

DO YOUR HOMEWORK. Only those on the front lines of free speech
know which bullets are the most lethal. Be aware and keep track of
the specific problems the law imposes on your everyday life as a
writer or speaker. Are there persistent problems in gaining access
to certain types of meetings or documents? Are local judges abus-
ing the right to hold in chambers conferences during trials? Are
your own lawyers, out of fear of libel suits, consistently advising
you to withhold information that the public needs to know? The
answers to such questions are the fodder of law making; without
them barriers to free speech multiply unopposed.

The truth is this: If citizens, especially the more earnest writers
and speakers among them, are to benefit from a legal landscape
shaped to maximize free expression, now, more than ever, they
must shape it for themselves. They cannot afford to sit on the side-
lines while politicians make points bashing the press.

As for the press, many news organizations, as a matter of principle, will not make campaign contributions. This principle has
come under growing fire as politics has become increasingly
influenced by big-spending political action committees. Whether
those who favor free speech should begin paying politicians for the
right to speak out against them is a debatable proposition. Even
with a PAC, however, and most certainly without one, the future
of free speech depends on informed public support. No one is better equipped to defend free speech than those who have most to
lose by its demise.

Appendix A

THE STRUCTURE OF LAW

THE PEOPLE (really, it was the states) conceded some (but not all) of the power to govern to the federal government's three branches. The Constitution is the document that defines the powers given to the federal government. Among its most striking features are the strict limitations placed on the exercise of those powers, limitations that have been interpreted and reinterpreted by generations of federal and state judges.

The states also have constitutions, which, like the federal government's, are more difficult to change than statutory law, usually requiring some form of popular initiative or consent. State constitutions, too, are subject to endless rounds of judicial scrutiny, making the task of predicting the meaning of even the hoariest constitutional provisions something of a crapshoot for lawyers who lack clairvoyance.

Constitutions set only the most basic ground rules. The legislatures, ranging from Congress down to the lowliest municipal water board, probably have enacted several dozens of new statutory provisions since you last picked up this book. The braying of purported conservatives has been unavailing in holding off the spread of the government's tentacles into each crevice of modern life. At the leading edge of the proliferation of government power is the enemy Pogo so aptly identified: we, the people, demanding that every wrong be offset by a new regulatory scheme and clamoring for lawyers to invoke all the majesty of their writs and *whereases* to make sure everyone gets theirs, even if it means sue, sue, sue.

To sue is to ask a court to use the power of government to compel or halt the doing of acts, mostly acts that involve paying money. To prevail, the *plaintiff*, the person or entity bringing the suit, must show that some legal right has been violated or threatened by the actions of the person named in the suit as the *defendant. Criminal actions* are lawsuits in which the state is the plaintiff; thus, such actions typically are styled "*People* v. *Smith*" or "*Texas* v. *Jones*." The state may be a party to a *civil suit* as well, either as a defendant or a plaintiff, but most often the parties are individuals or private entities, like business corporations, involved in disputes about contractual rights or tort claims. A *tort* is roughly analogous to the civil version of a crime; many acts that constitute crimes are also actionable as torts. For example, the victim's family may sue a murderer for economic loss tied to the slaying. Libel and the several varieties of invasion of privacy are torts, wrongful acts that result in injury to others.

Torts, like crimes, may be defined in the *statutes* of a state. In California, for example, the civil code defines libel. In other states, however, there may be no statutory definition; the courts instead rely on the *common law* to determine whether the state recognizes the tort, and, if so, how it is defined. The tort of false-light invasion of privacy, for example, is recognized in the common law of some states, but not all. Even if there is a statutory definition, the courts must look to "common" or "decisional" law for help in applying the definition to the specific facts of a case. Common law is imbedded in the published decisions of a state's courts, sometimes reaching back to origins in the law of Great Britain. A state whose courts have never ruled on an issue may borrow from the decisions of other states to answer a "question of first impression." Plaintiffs sometimes may choose among the courts of two or more *jurisdictions,* that is among two or more states or between state court or federal court, in deciding where to file a lawsuit.

A tort lawsuit begins with the filing of a *complaint* with the court clerk of the appropriate jurisdiction, who collects a filing fee, assigns a number and issues a *summons.* The plaintiff must then *serve* the summons and a copy of the complaint on the defendant. Service rules vary from jurisdiction to jurisdiction. Most require at least an attempt at personal service before permitting service by mail or other means. In some jurisdictions, service must be made within a relatively brief period after filing; in others, the time for service is open-ended.

The complaint sets forth the plaintiff's explanation of how the defendant's actions meet the definition of a tort. Some complaints are very detailed, reading like a medieval narrative of the horrors wrought upon the hapless plaintiff by the reckless conduct of the morally corrupt and thoroughly disreputable defendant. Other complaints are legalistic formulas giving the ordinary reader scarcely a clue as to the alleged offense. Many states encourage the filing of standardized complaints, using court-approved forms that require the plaintiff merely to check boxes and fill in a few blanks.

Once the plaintiff serves the summons and complaint, the defendant has a limited time in which to file a response, usually thirty days. Exactly how many days and how those days are counted vary widely, but the defendant should get legal advice immediately and prepare for defense. Failure to respond to a complaint in time can lead to consequences as drastic as an entry of judgment by *default,* requiring you to pay everything requested by the plaintiff, without having an opportunity to explain your defense.

The response to a complaint usually will be either an *answer* or a *motion to dismiss.* Other names may be used; for example, a motion to dismiss still is known in some states as a *demurrer.* A motion to dismiss is a way of asking the court to rule that, regardless of what the evidence ultimately may show, the complaint does not state a claim.

Motions to dismiss often are filed, but, if granted, usually only force the plaintiff to rewrite, and improve, the complaint. An answer, on the other hand, disputes the complaint's contentions and sets forth legal reasons (known as *affirmative defenses*) why the conduct described by the plaintiff does not provide a right to recover damages. Once an answer is on file, the lawsuit is at issue and the real fun begins, although usually excruciatingly slowly.

Much of the pain of modern lawsuits results from an innovation designed to make the process more fair, the requirement that both sides show all their factual cards to the opposition before trial. This process of exchanging information is known as *discovery.* The two primary components of discovery are depositions and interrogatories.

A *deposition* is an oral examination of a witness or a party to a lawsuit taken under oath and recorded, either stenographically or electronically. "Trial lawyers," those who specialize in litigating disputes, spend only a small fraction of their time with judges and juries; they while away most of their days in depositions.

In major lawsuits, there may be dozens of lawyers participating in each deposition, though in most cases, one will be "taking" the deposition (asking most of the questions) and another will be "defending" it (raising objections or trying to block certain questions). Depositions typically occur in a lawyer's office. If disputes arise, and they often do, a judge may officiate, but only after more hours of time are wasted preparing and responding to written motions explaining the dispute for the judge's benefit. Most testimony is transcribed and stacked waist-deep in lawyers' offices, but only a small portion may be entered into the formal court file.

Interrogatories and their relatives, such as *production demands* (written requests for documents and physical evidence, not petitions for motion picture sequels) or r*equests for admission,* seek information in documentary form.

Sometimes, the product of discovery is so massive that warehouses overflow with it and software companies make a tidy profit designing programs to index and search it all, increasingly from portable computers brought into the courtroom at trial.

As discovery goes on, the lawyers may present arguments to persuade the judge to resolve the case without a trial or to narrow the issues or limit the evidence. Such arguments take the form of *motions.* Motions are requests for judicial rulings. The most important is the motion for *summary judgment.* Either party may bring a summary judgment motion at any time after the answer is filed until a specified period before the trial date (in most jurisdictions, thirty to sixty days). Unlike a motion to dismiss, a summary judgment motion is not limited to technical legal issues, but may ask a judge to consider evidence, or, what is more important, lack of evidence. For example, if there is no evidence that the defendant's car was involved in the accident, the defendant may ask that the accident victim's suit be "summarily" dismissed, that is, dismissed without a trial.

The summary judgment motion is an extremely useful tool for defendants in libel suits, because the evidentiary burdens facing libel plaintiffs are quite high. Often a judge decides *as a matter of law* that there are no *triable issues of fact,* and dismisses the lawsuit.

Few tort cases make it all the way to trial through the Byzantine maze of discovery and pretrial motions. Judges dismiss a few on summary judgment motions. Most are settled by the parties, who, worn down or enlightened by the process, become convinced that the expense and the risk of loss are sufficient to justify compromising their differences. Defenders of the American judicial system see this process as a salutary feature of our way of life that allows the resolution of vast differences at reasonable cost and with a minimum of violence. Others see the entire system as a Dickensian scheme for enriching lawyers and encouraging litigation. Fortunately, resolving that particular dispute is not an aim of this book. As it happens, settlements are relatively rare in First Amendment cases; most libel suits, for example, end in nominal victory for the defendant, even though at great cost.

Judicial rulings and jury verdicts may be *appealed*. In most jurisdictions, there is at least one appeal open to all litigants. In addition, there may be a second appeal available at the discretion of the reviewing court. In the federal system, the trial court is the United States District Court. If a district court judge dismisses a complaint, the losing party may ask the United States Court of Appeals for the relevant circuit (there are eleven judicial circuits known by their circuit numbers, plus the Federal Circuit and the District of Columbia Circuit) to review the decision. This first level of appeal is a review *as of right:* if asked, the Court of Appeals must review the decision.

The loser in the Court of Appeals may ask for a review by the Supreme Court. The Supreme Court, however, need not grant review in most cases; it selects only those cases that raise issues of significant general interest or otherwise tickle the fancies of four or more justices. To request a review by the Supreme Court, a party usually must file a *petition for certiorari.* If the Court grants "cert," both parties have the opportunity to present written briefs and oral arguments.

Appeals as of right are available only after entry of *final judgment.* A judge's ruling granting a summary judgment motion is final, since it ends the lawsuit, but a denial of a summary judgment is not final; the lawsuit continues to trial. Appellate review of "nonfinal" rulings may be requested, but most often is denied by the appellate court without oral arguments, or, even, an opportunity for written response from the other side. Such *interlocutory appeals* are important in First Amendment cases because timeliness is often a critical element, such as, for example, when a journalist is cooling her heels in jail after refusing to identify a source or a judge blocks a news organization from printing information about a current controversy. Even if an appeal as of right is possible, it may take many months or years to work its way through the appeal docket, while an interlocutory appeal may be acted on in days or even hours.

Appellate judges are bound to make decisions of *law* not of *fact.* Since they do not have the benefit of the witnesses testifying in front of them, they usually may not reweigh the evidence and substitute their judgments for those of the *trier of fact,* usually a jury, though sometimes it is a judge. The primary role of appellate judges is to make sure juries and trial judges follow legal rules and procedures. This often leads to confusion about the meaning of appellate decisions, especially those reversing a trial court's grant of summary judgment. When a summary judgment decision is before an appellate court, the issue is not who should win the lawsuit. The only question is whether the trial judge erred in not allowing the case to go to trial. Because of the frequency of summary judgment in First Amendment cases, appellate courts occasionally reverse summary judgment rulings won by media organizations or other defendants asserting First Amendment rights. Such a reversal may be misinterpreted as a finding that the defendant is guilty of the allegations made against him; the reality is more complex.

A similar misinterpretation afflicts the Supreme Court's decisions to "deny cert," or refuse to review cases. Denying review is not the same as upholding the decision of the lower court. Most "cert" denials do reflect the Supreme Court's view, or, at least, the view of the young clerks who brief the justices, that the decision of the lower court is unexceptionable, but many times certiorari is denied out of expedience. The Court does not have time to examine every disputed decision.

Appendix B

RESOURCES

ORGANIZATIONS

THE REPORTERS COMMITTEE for Freedom of the Press is a tireless, if chronically underfunded, advocate of First Amendment education and reform. Its periodic compilations of reports on legal issues affecting the press, *The News Media and the Law,* and its handbooks, especially its guide to the Freedom of Information Act, are invaluable and cheap. Lawyers are on staff who can answer questions from working journalists. Write to them at 1101 Wilson Blvd., Suite 1910, Arlington, VA 22209 or call (703) 807-2100. Better still, send a check for twenty-five dollars; you'll get a year's worth of *The News Media and the Law* and order forms for other publications.

The Society of Professional Journalists also has a noble tradition of leadership on First Amendment issues. Its headquarters are at 16 S. Jackson Street, Greencastle, IN 46135-0077, (317) 653-3333.

The Radio-Television News Directors Association is a leader on issues affecting electronic journalists, especially court access. The headquarters are at 1000 Connecticut Ave. NW, Suite 615, Washington, DC 20036, (202) 659-6510.

A sampling of other organizations that include First Amendment leadership among their services to members are:

American Society of Newspaper Editors, P.O. Box 4090, Reston, VA 22090-1700, (703) 648-1144.

Libel Defense Resource Center, 404 Park Avenue South, 16th floor, New York City, NY 10016, (202) 889-2306.

National Association of Broadcasters, 1771 N St. NW, Washington, DC 20036, (202) 429-5430.

National Newspaper Association, 1525 Wilson Blvd., Suite 550, Arlington VA 22209, (703) 907-7902.

Newspaper Association of America, The Newspaper Center,

11600 Sunrise Valley Drive, Reston, VA 22091-1412, (703) 648-1000.

Almost every state has several associations whose interests include free speech issues. Many publish excellent handbooks on their states' laws and some have staff lawyers who provide advice to members. Scores are listed in the associations sections of the *Editor and Publisher Yearbook* and *Broadcasting Yearbook,* both of which can be found in public libraries. Representatives include:

California Newspaper Publishers Association, 1225 Eighth Street, Sacramento, CA 95814-4809, (916) 443-5991.

Pennsylvania Newspaper Publishers Association, 2717 N. Front Street, Harrisburg, PA 17110, (717) 234-4067.

Illinois Press Association, 701 S. Grand Avenue West, Springfield, IL 62704, (217) 523-5092.

An insurance company that offers libel coverage to news media organizations as well as book publishers and individuals is: Media Professional Insurance, Inc., Two Pershing Square, Suite 800, 2300 Main Street, Kansas City, MO 64108, (816) 471-6118. The Libel Defence Resource Center can provide names of others.

BOOKS

A number of excellent books for lawyers cover First Amendment topics. Unfortunately, most of the books cited here carry a lawyerlike price tag. Fortunately, most cities and many courthouses have law libraries where these and other works may be consulted.

One of the most comprehensive is *Media Law,* by Rex S. Heinke, Washington: Bureau of National Affairs, 1994. (BNA is at 1231 25th Street NW, Washington, DC 20037.)

An invaluable resource is the *Media Law Reporter,* a weekly "advance sheet" service, also by BNA, that carries the full text of most media- and First Amendment–related court decisions. Its numbers are collected in bound volumes that date back to the 1970s. It is available in many law libraries, or, for those with an inheritance, by subscription for $933 per year.

Equally invaluable and less expensive are the course books for the

Practising Law Institute's annual program on communications law, chaired by James C. Goodale. PLI also sponsors other programs on media law topics, especially their seminar on libel litigation, chaired by Richard Winfield. For catalogs and ordering information, call PLI at (212) 765-5700.

Libel and privacy are authoritatively covered in:

Libel, Slander and Related Problems, 2d ed., by Robert D. Sack and Sandra S. Baron, New York: Practising Law Institute, 1994.

Libel and Privacy, 2d ed., by Bruce W. Sanford, Englewood Cliffs, N.J.: Aspen Law & Business, 1993. (Aspen may be reached at (201) 894-8484.)

For copyright, as well as issues of particular interest to books and magazines, see *The Publishing Law Handbook,* second edition, by E. Gabriel Perle and John Taylor Williams, also published by Aspen.

One of the few general-interest books that takes a comprehensive look at the history and meaning of the First Amendment is Nat Hentoff's *The First Freedom* (New York: Delacorte Press, 1980). There are many books for general readers that tell the story of particular cases. Some worthy samples include:

Minnesota Rag, Fred W. Friendly, New York: Random House, 1981. *Near* v. *Minnesota,* the case in which the Supreme Court acknowledged the application of the First Amendment to state laws, arose out of the odoriferous activities of a Minnesota misanthrope.

Make No Law, Anthony Lewis, New York: Random House, 1991. The definitive account of *New York Times* v. *Sullivan.* Includes the text of the Supreme Court's opinion.

Coals of Fire, Thomas B. Littlewood, Carbondale, Ill.: Southern Illinois University Press, 1988. How the *Alton Telegraph* suffered a $10 million libel judgment and never got a story.

CASES

For those who want to sample the law at the source, the citations to court decisions listed below will provide an introduction. For many more, see the tables of cases included in the books cited above. Two law school casebooks that include excerpts from these and many other cases are Donald M. Gillmor, Jerome Barron, Todd F. Simon, and Herbert A. Terry, *Mass Communication Law: Cases and Comment,* fifth edition (West Publishing Co., St. Paul, Minn.) and Marc A. Franklin and David A. Anderson, *Cases and Materials on Mass Media Law,* fifth edition (Foundation Press, Westbury, N.Y.).

U.S. Supreme Court cases are those with a "U.S." in the citation, which is to the official *United States Reports.* Federal court of appeals cases are cited to "F.2d," a segment of the West Publishing Company's National Reporter System. Decisions of state courts have an abbreviation for the state somewhere in the citation. For each case where one is available, citations to the *Media Law Reporter* also are included. Many general-interest libraries carry the decisions of the United States Supreme Court. For the others, you'll need a law library.

Constitutional Libel

New York Times v. *Sullivan* (First Amendment limits common law libel action by public official), 376 U.S. 254, 1 MLR 1527 (1964).

Gertz v. *Welch* (Constitution requires all libel plaintiffs to prove some degree of fault), 418 U.S. 323, 1 MLR 1633 (1974).

Ollman v. *Evans* (statement of opinion protected by Constitution), 750 F.2d 970, 11 MLR 1433 (D.C. Cir. 1984).

Masson v. *New Yorker* (error in quoting plaintiff may support libel claim), 111 S.Ct. 2419, 18 MLR 2241 (1991).

Common Law Libel

Crump v. *Beckley Newspapers, Inc.* (applying modern common law principles to a libel claim), 320 S.E.2d 70, 10 MLR 2225 (W. Va. 1984).

False Light

Time v. *Hill* (Constitution limits false light claims), 385 U.S. 374, 1 MLR 1791 (1967).

Intentional Infliction of Emotional Distress

Hustler Magazine v. *Falwell* (Constitution limits claims arising out of speech, whether phrased as libel or other torts), 485 U.S. 46, 14 MLR 2281 (1988).

Promissory Estoppel

Cohen v. *Cowles Media Co.* (promise to conceal a source's identity may be enforceable), 501 U.S. 663, 18 MLR 2273 (1991).

Private Facts

Melvin v. *Reid* (the *Red Kimono* case, holding that passage of time may limit right to disseminate otherwise public facts), 112 Cal.App. 285 (Cal. Ct. App. 1931).

Florida Star v. *B.J.F.* (reversing judgment for publication of rape victim's name), 491 U.S. 524, 16 MLR 1801 (1989).

News Gathering

Dietemann v. *Time* (using hidden cameras and recorders in target's home office held an intrusion), 449 F.2d 245, 1 MLR 2417 (9th Cir. 1971).

Galella v. *Onassis* (aggressive acts of pursuit and endangerment to obtain photographs held an intrusion), 487 F.2d 986, 1 MLR 2425 (2d Cir. 1973).

Prior Restraints

Nebraska Press Association v. *Stuart* (overruling gag order against press comment on murder prosecution), 427 U.S. 539, 1 MLR 1064 (1976).

Associated Press v. *U.S. District Court* (DeLorean) (overruling order sealing files in criminal case), 705 F.2d 1143, 9 MLR 1617 (9th Cir. 1983).

New York Times v. *United States* (government not entitled to block publication of Pentagon Papers), 403 U.S. 713, 1 MLR 1031 (1971).

Access to Courts

Press Enterprise Co. v. *Superior Court* (Press-Enterprise II)(preliminary hearing in criminal case presumed to be open), 478 U.S. 1, 13 MLR 1001 (1986).

United States v. *Smith* (denying access to sidebar conferences but requiring release of transcripts), 787 F.2d 111, 12 MLR 1935 (3d Cir. 1986).

Publicker Industries v. *Cohen* (First Amendment requires access to civil proceedings), 733 F.2d 1059, 10 MLR 1777 (3d Cir. 1984).

Access to Judicial Records

Nixon v. *Warner Communications* (acknowledging common law right of access to records of criminal proceedings), 435 U.S. 589 (1978), 3 MLR 2074 (1978).

Reporter's Privilege

Branzburg v. *Hayes,* (divided court lays foundation for First Amendment protection from reporter subpoenas), 408 U.S. 665, 1 MLR 2617 (1972).

Farr v. *Pitchess* (acknowledging First Amendment right for reporters to refuse testimony), 522 F.2d 464 (9th Cir. 1975).

Property Rights

Zacchini v. *Scripps-Howard Broadcasting Co.* (human cannonball's "right of publicity" supports claim against television station that aired film of his act), 433 U.S. 562, 2 MLR 2089 (1977).

American Geophysical Union v. *Texaco* (researcher's photocopying of journal articles not fair use), 37 F.3d 881 (2d Cir. 1994).